I0202194

HOW PHILOSOPHY COULD SAVE THE WORLD

Vernon Molloy

Table of Contents

Foreword

In 2015, I published *Modern Problems, Ancient Perspectives*. The book is available on Amazon.com and Amazon.ca; or from the trunk of whatever vehicle I happen to be driving.

I carry copies in case I come across someone in need of transcendental solutions. Transcendental solutions are wonderful. As soon as you come across them, you know they are true.

There are two reasons to read books. The first is that they are worth reading and you would otherwise miss out. The second is that they are not worth reading and you miss not seeing this. You may think: "Not reading something not worth reading" sounds like a good idea. This overlooks the fun of identifying an author's confusion. Surely this amounts to a serious opportunity!

There is one thing more. If a reader sees the error of my ways, has a chuckle and then generously extricates me from my confusion, I also get to be a winner.

Transcendentally speaking, I see no downside to you making the best purchase of our lives.

After the 'book launch', I took *Modern Times, Ancient Perspectives* to the philosophy department at Queen's University, Kingston, Ontario. In 1985, they gave me the benefit of the doubt in the guise of an MA. I now hoped they might consider this book as the nucleus of a PhD project.

I was encouraged (or at least allowed) to make an application, which I submitted in January 2016.

HOW PHILOSOPHY COULD

The application began with a call to philosophical arms, which I include here in lieu of a keynote speaker.

I include a few items from *Modern Problems, Ancient Solutions* and sketch the moral implications of Einstein's relativity theory. An item about a hockey mother culled from my diary twenty years ago leads to a discussion of the role of sports and democracy in the modern world.

The book focuses upon realism and commonsense claims about consciousness, agency and realism.

Although these issues may seem far removed from anything that matters, I think they are deeply involved in attitudes and projects driving our once-shiny world over a cliff.

Philosophers Spawn a World

Call me old-fashioned but I think the world a few thousand years ago seemed younger to people at the time. I'm sure that hardly anything going on today is as exciting as being alive was during the springtime of understanding.

In those 'good old days' information and socializing opportunities were hard to come by. The result was that many people remained curious, questioning and childishly-wise. Cultural accomplishments—languages, oral traditions, technologies—had accumulated sufficiently that big-picture issues could be talked about. They had not mounted so high that nothing remained to discuss.

We know this because these small populations initiated the cosmologies, myths and sciences now regarded as common-sense and realism.

In those days—celebrated in Western nations as Hellenism, the pre-Socratic era, Plato and Aristotle—people had the world for their oyster. Philosophers were thick on the ground. They rambled around muttering to themselves and buttonholing anyone who would listen. The resulting conversations planted seeds that would grow into corporations, nations and the modern world.

Ironically, these successes diminished the sense of wonder that made them possible. After deputizing scientists and artists to do all their heavy-lifting, philosophy shriveled into an arcane activity practiced in broom closets and remote corners of universities.

To be sure, philosophers continued sharpening

logical tools, confident that they would be welcomed soon enough. They continued pondering moral and epistemological questions no one else cared about. Not noticing their emeritus status, they soldiered on, hoping to corral some eminent truth and repair their reputation.

This has not—and cannot—happen. Philosophical standpoints define what count as truth. Such benchmarks can be argued about but they cannot be tested to determine whether they are correctly situated. The idea that they could 'progress' is equally oxymoronic.

A second difficulty is that every 'candidate insight' triggers an internecine frenzy. Philosophers attempt to overturn—or at least improve—every point of view they come across. Since they lack Large Hadron Colliders to investigate perplexing questions, perpetual, mutual sniping is their only tool.

The result is that almost all the important questions remain on the table. This is actually an accomplishment that should be celebrated. It sets the stage for what must now be accomplished.

Of course, remarkable insights have occurred along the way. John Rawls' theory of justice and Immanuel Kant's universalizability test come to mind. Ludwig Wittgenstein discarded his own picture theory of language (that earned him a doctorate at Cambridge University) to challenge commonsense notions in his later years, in ways. Philosophers, psychologists and linguists are still mining the results for insights.

The result? No epiphanies, no conclusions, only increasingly subtle questions. What's valuable about not 'being able' to come to conclusions? The answer lies in the alternative.

SAVE THE WORLD

Politicians, corporations, nations ... have no
difficulty coming to and acting upon decisions.
They harvest resources recklessly. They ride
rough-shod across everything.

I think this means wars, global warming, global
poverty ... reflect philosophers' historical
failures to challenge, indict, publicize,
excoriate ... their doubt-free progeny—the
scientists, engineers and rationalists John
Raulston Saul called Voltaire's bastards.

Scepticism is what philosophers are good at.
They have kept one another scoreless for
thousands of years! This skepticism must be
expanded. We must all become philosophers.
This is the only way to restore curiosity,
optimism and lack of certainty to a moribund
world.

Consciousness' Modest Role

The great majority of men ... work gradually at eclipsing their ethical and ethical-religious comprehension, which would lead them out into decisions and conclusions that their lower nature does not much care for.

Soren Kierkegaard

Quite a few have suggested that I spend too much time fussing about the nature of consciousness. This puzzles me because conscious episodes are all we have to talk about. How can it not be interesting to think about how and why they occur? There are many questions: what is the relationship between consciousness and its contents? Which comes first? Are the contents of consciousness and consciousness itself like chickens and eggs, constantly creating and shading into one another?

In my experience—and I assume this holds for others—thoughts and conclusions flow from previous thoughts, from awarenesses traceable to external events, from conversations, or they simply pop into awareness the way creative people frequently describe.

I think this spontaneity is the reason we have been getting consciousness wrong—an error I think that has been having grave consequences. A great deal turns upon what function consciousness is 'performing', upon whether consciousness is intrinsically active or, as I propose, passive.

To put my card on the table, I suggest that conscious episodes function the way blackboards and shopping lists facilitate communications within and among conscious beings. This 'assistance' may involve 'notes to self' or to other people, but it remains passive, the way reminder notes require someone looking at them to function.

After decades accepting the common view that consciousness is the seat of agency and person-hood, I came to understand that this could not be true. Intuitively and logically, consciousness is not able to act upon or engage with its contents.

Like awareness of sounds, sights and feelings, conscious episodes are generated by cognitive events, not the other way around.

This modest claim replaces the notion that consciousness is active or efficacious in and of itself. We believe consciousness brings something to the party that does not exist when human beings are too young to be 'fully conscious', to not, as Catholics say, have reached the age of reason. When we sleeping, drugged or knocked out we are deemed similarly innocent.

We leverage this claim into the belief that consciousness differentiates human beings from other forms of life, that consciousness is the catalyst transforming behaviour into conduct. Thus, Kierkegaard's comment assumes, implies, accepts ... that consciousness can choose to "work gradually at eclipsing ... comprehensions".

Why consciousness would not obliterate problematic comprehensions instantly instead of grinding them down is not clear. What is clear is that the 'eclipsing' Kierkegaard speaks of involves the claim that consciousness proceeds ex nihilo, that its contents and deliverances cannot be tracked back to previous causes, including earlier decisions of the person whose decision it is.

9

Free will and choosing talk also depend upon the claim that consciousness judges and interprets its own contents. This is like saying rulers can measure themselves, see whether they fall long or short and then, presumably, make adjustments! This is what it means to speak of individuals performing (or not performing) acts for which they can be praised or blamed. The litmus test is always whether individuals are conscious, 'in possession of their faculties' and have sufficient time to form a premeditated intention. Thus, a guilty mind (intention to perform some criminal act) must exist prior to the act being performed: *mens rea* before or during *actus reus*.

Although rarely stated, a similar analysis applies to apportioning praise, rewards and financial outcomes.

In spite of dubious credentials, free will claims are difficult to challenge. Although there is a premonition that everything will eventually be explained, until this happens we keep moving the conscious agency claim around so that it is always outside of whatever behaviour is on the table.

Alternatively, we acknowledge that deterministic explanations might eventually explain everything, but insist that nothing turns on this. We say: "Yes, but look at what we get up to!", then carry on as if agency and morality talk made as much sense as it did when supernatural entities were thick on the ground.

The irony is that human beings are more likely to become persons (autonomous moral and rational creatures) as soon as we stop insisting that we already are. The recipe is as homely as the noses on our faces. The most important ingredient is recognizing that person-hood is not a guaranteed birthright. The second is realizing that, while person-hood is possible, it must be achieved. Like gardens, persons must be grown.

It is impossible to say what a person is. As soon as a definition is struck, the next person we come across may have become so by clambering over it. However, it is possible to say what persons are not. Hitlers, Kim Jong-uns and their goose-stepping buffoons, are not persons in any interesting sense of the word. The chanting, gesticulating, genuflecting congregations in churches and Walmart stores are not persons either. The chances of coming across persons is higher in refugee camps than in those responsible for refugee camps.

The business of growing persons cannot be summarized. However a bit of house-cleaning is possible.

If human beings had not begun the process of understanding by claiming that consciousness is active and efficacious, I think we would have evolved more useful views of ourselves and one another. I think we would have a different sense of the world. For example, the phenomenal world (full of private images and imagined proceedings) would not have automatically transformed into 'common sense' claims involving an external world.

As soon as what is going on is understood in such partitioned ways, confusion and divisiveness is baked into everything that follows. Realism is one explanation of the phenomenal world. There are many possibilities however. Perhaps realism would not have been settled upon had it not been presented as axiomatically self-evident. For example, if elements, objects, entities, events ... are understood as private images in subjective lives, there is no reason to regard images as more than figures of speech summarizing and conveying information.

Thus, it is convenient—far too convenient—to organize populations under quasi-object headings: liberals, conservatives, Protestants, Catholics, rich, poor, communists, capitalists ... These measures allow stump speeches without having to reinvent ideological wheels. Robust entreaties, vigorous disputes, bar room brawls and military adventures need not waste time discussing what the fuss is all about.

As well, thinking about what is going on in shorthand ways, in terms of things, entities, persons ..., has survival value. One of the reasons the digital age and the INTERNET expanded so astonishingly is that programmers and users find graphical user interfaces (GUI's) computationally liberating. I think we have been down this road before. Thinking about experiences in terms of objects, entities and persons is advantageous for the same reason graphical user interfaces (and second life avatars) eliminate the need for terminal screens and command strings. The consciousness model sketched here proposes that things, entities, persons ... are best understood as GUI's reducing computational burdens and response times.

The rest of the story involves the 'hard problem' of consciousness. I propose a bottom-up explanation. Reflexes and conditioned responses evolved into a capacity for conscious episodes. Conscious episodes are reflexes and conditioned responses stretched out until they encompass seconds, minutes, hours ... instead of microseconds. The capacity for conscious experiences is thus an emergent phenomenon, not a supernatural endowment or evolutionary breakthrough.

SAVE THE WORLD

I will set this out in more detail further along but the important issue is that the notion consciousness as a choice-generating engine sets the stage for an amazing ploy. By regarding consciousness as source of indictable or praiseworthy decisions, we identify an inscrutable aspect of our own being as responsible for what we get up to.

To be sure, we often find ourselves resorting to multiple villains when scapegoating just one face becomes implausible. This was how responsibility of millions of Germans for Second World War events was transferred to twenty three *war criminals* tried at Nuremberg. There was not twenty four because Hitler had killed himself—a fact that improved his scapegoat value because self-condemning, self-punishing villains are able to shoulder enormous responsibilities. Cultures everywhere do everything they can to encourage such volunteers.

Scapegoating was also what Freud was on about when he developed a model 'spreading responsibility' for human behaviour among id, ego and superego. This trinity of players mitigated personal culpability even as it allowed Dr. Freud to take credit for his insights!

This is also what Descartes had in mind with his account of mental (supernatural, spiritual) substances interacting with the material world by way of pineal glands.

Culturally-embedded notions about scapegoating is what lawyers play with when they argue for or against Murder in the First Degree. The moral is clear even if the morality is suspect: if responsibility for heinous behaviour cannot be vested in a subset of the human population by way of *mens rea* talk, responsibility would flow through to families, communities and other generative circumstances.

In this story, the German nation would have been less able to shake off responsibility for the Second World War by offering up a handful of miscreants. The fact that these individuals were malignant in their own right made the scapegoating trope all the more effective. The question that remained unasked is whether the German population and culture had anything to do with the genesis of these malignant individuals.

In general, I suggest that the conscious episodes referred to by lawyers are the tips of generative icebergs. We see such icebergs forming all the time. No matter how desperate their circumstances, children and adolescents are interested in and curious about what is going on around them. They have not yet been rendered into individuals equipped with cognitive 'spam filters' deflecting, dissolving, dismissing ... information streaming in from whatever culture they happen to live in.

(I refer to the world before television, smart phones and the INTERNET rendered locally sourced conscious episodes occasional echoes of inner-directed, self-subsisting forms of life.)

The original function of cognitive filters (including permissible cognitive dissonance and habituation functions) was to diminish the need to pay attention to recurring events and problems. This was an excellent plan as long as human beings lived in circumstances where new individuals and novel problems kept turning up. Unfortunately, urban life—the de facto womb within which more and more human beings find themselves—contains few problems that cannot be solved with flicking switches, flushing toilets or calling 911.

As a consequence, human beings are enjoying

SAVE THE WORLD

fewer and fewer conscious moments. This is also why time seems to go faster as one ages. Fewer events requiring conscious episodes mean fewer memories.

In fairness, a shrinking conscious life contains an ironic benefit. A disengaged, myopic life tests the quality of one's economic and political circumstances. If urbanites can survive without paying much attention to what is going on, then what is going on must be wholesome.

The downside is that, in the absence of conscious episodes, we may not notice our excellent lives, and what kind of excellent life is that?

To be sure, should mischief become unmistakable, alarms will still sound, but perhaps too late for nearby people. Of course, even dead canaries can serve a purpose. If enough people come to grief because communities and corporations are infected with toxic proceedings, remedies sometimes get enacted. The tobacco industry provides an example. Harms suffered by millions of smokers led to constraints upon advertising and no-smoking legislation.

These are deep waters. Such repairs can themselves become toxic. Legislation, surveillance, interdiction ... sanction— sometimes demand— public submission and dependence. These results can further erode the incidence of conscious episodes.

Emergent Life

The falling off of the frequency of conscious episodes implies a corresponding diminution in the proportion of human beings qualifying as persons. The number of individuals whose behaviour can be predicted—i.e., who fail the *persons* litmus test—correlates with institutional, corporate and government control over ordinary responsibilities.

This is not all we should be worried about. Nations, corporations and institutions have agendas that go beyond the wishes of voters, workers or consumers. These organizations are regularly spoken of as creatures with volitions and agendas. This is usually done metaphorically, as a hedge against accusations of anthropomorphism. Even so, corporations are already *legal persons*, and this status is regularly fleshed out with new powers and prerogatives.

Corporations, institutions and nations enjoy powerful advantages over the people constituting and ostensibly controlling their activities. Corporations are immortal. They can grow to any size and they certainly develop organs of assimilation, defence and defecation.[1]

The issue of corporate intentionality is complicated because the activities of nations and corporations appear to flow from (and not through) the citizens, employees, customers ... constituting their being. What is also overlooked in the belief that corporations aggregate the wishes of component individuals is that organized proceedings have emergent properties. They spawn outcomes

---

1   http://www.npr.org/2014/07/28/335288388/
     when-did-companies-become-people-
     excavating-the-legal-evolution

greater than or different from outcomes one would expect adding up the intentions of constituent individuals. In addition, these outcomes participate in unfathomable knock-on events. Since these further events could not have been part of the intentions of employees, customers or citizens, it is fair to say that they reflect the intentions of organizations. If you object that organizations lack consciousness and therefore any capacity to form intentions, I argue below that human intentionality is similarly unconscious in its origin and in almost all of its proceedings.

An example of an emergent property: hydrogen (a flammable gas) combines with oxygen (necessary for combustion) and forms H20 water—a compound with properties not readily predicted by examining the properties of its its components, yet one exceptionally good at putting out fires!

A central characteristic of emergent phenomena is that they cannot be predicted by examining the central tendencies, wishes, votes ... of the atoms, cells, networks of cells, citizens ... comprising creatures, corporations, or nations.

Your and my participation in corporations and nations is both prior to and constitutive of what they get up to. We are in no position to 'control' outcomes by assessing and choosing courses of actions. We are instead like the proverbial donkey trying to reach a tuft of hay dangling from a pole attached to its back. Our sense of forward is dictated by our sense of hay, no matter which way we are headed. Even if we could manage 'dangling hay' workarounds, we could not 'manage' the events these successes would spawn. We have no way of knowing what they will consist of until they have been experienced.

This simple story challenges free will and agency claims. Significantly,this challenge remains even if consciousness is efficacious the way common sense proposes.

To some extent we understand ourselves in emergent terms. We recognize that our existence depends upon synergies among millions or billions of body parts, cells, gut bacteria ... We know (and take pride in!) the obvious fact that what we get up to could not be anticipated by summing up the agendas of our component bits. This emergent argument provides the wiggle room we exploit with free will and conscious choice talk.

The important question is not whether corporations and nations are under human control, but whether they are more usefully understood as emergent events in the same way conscious episodes are more usefully understood as emergent events.

If so, urbanization, specialization and globalization are creating another dilemma. Corporations and nations may be taking advantage of the dwindling number of locally-sourced conscious episodes to gain further sway and become more autonomous.

Already billions of conscious episodes occur every day in movie theatres, hockey arenas and on television screens. Our lives are increasingly 'cloud based'. Our capacity to have conscious episodes—which sets the stage for personal achievements and understandings—is being co-opted by corporations and nations. The ability to function as persons is being bartered away for the convenience of having lives organized and needs and wants met without the need for pesky conscious episodes. (This is the theme of Aldous Huxley's *Brave New World* published in 1932.)

SAVE THE WORLD

This willingness to outsource and automate responsibilities requiring conscious episodes might seem surprising. However, I have come to understand that experiencing a conscious episode is rather like being in a house with a smoke detector sounding. Our instinct is to find out what is wrong so we can resume whatever state we were in before the alarm went off. We instinctively do whatever it takes can to make sure the alarm does not sound again. Technologies amplify this inclination thousands of times over.

Certainly, episodic consciousness is not the halcyon life enjoyed in the womb. This is not how we understand Heaven either. Heaven is an eternal, serene contemplation of the Divine —an eternal, delicious slumber with never a pulse of alarm or requirement for attention.

On the other hand, if our destiny involves that other place, we have been warned to expect lots of conscious episodes as we sizzle endlessly on (or in) God's Divine Spit.

The moral is that conscious episodes appear to be something human beings avoid as often as possible. Conscious episodes signal that something out of the ordinary is occurring. Now that we are urbanized, organized and sophisticated, now that pretty much everything has been battened down, 'something out of the ordinary' is almost always bad news.

Whether corporations are emergent life forms is interesting to think about, but it is not the most important issue confronting human beings. The falling off of internally-sourced conscious episodes means that, when urbanized, specialized individuals conspire ('breathe together'), beneficial or destructive events can occur without anyone noticing.

19

HOW PHILOSOPHY COULD

Hitler's megalomania did not spread across Germany because his countrymen consciously considered his arguments and then voted for him. The German population's consciousness-capable minds became a medium of communication orchestrating similarly constituted 'individuals' into monstrous events.

With Hitler as focal point, conscious episodes in millions of Germans spontaneously organized into militant bigotry, Antisemitism and master race conceits coalesced in monstrous ways. The Second World War erupted, with Germany as its fulminating core.

The problem has not gone away. Antisemitism in Europe has increased in recent years. To be fair, most nations are reporting incidents more accurately than in the past. Because of this, it is not possible to make direct comparisons over time or among countries. Even so, things seem to be getting worse.

> Beginning in 2000, verbal attacks directed against Jews increased while incidents of vandalism (e.g. graffiti, fire bombings of Jewish schools, desecration of synagogues and cemeteries) surged. Physical assaults including beatings, stabbings and other violence against Jews in Europe increased markedly, in a number of cases resulting in serious injury and even death. Also troubling is a bias that spills over into Antisemitism in some of the left-of-centre press and among some intellectuals.[2]

How can this be recurring after causing so much torment and receiving so much

---

2   http://www.state.gov/j/drl/rls/40258.htm

condemnation in the last century alone? I suggest that when consciousness is displaced from its role transforming human beings into persons, it risks becoming a medium of communication among unconscious proceedings. This creates the possibility of unconscious elements in human beings communicating' and forming alliances. When these alliances become corporations, nations or armies, they develop momentum and intentions distinct from the agendas of constituent workers or citizens.

We have seen the devastation these (de facto) organisms are capable of, but have not taken the examples seriously. We continue to believe that corporations and nations rise out of the conscious choices of citizens and workers. We believe they come into existence by mutual public consent and are thereafter guided by 'invisible human hands' in marketplaces and governments.

We admire democratic forms of government because we believe conscious agents voting is the only legitimate source of political power and the only possible path to public well-being.

What if none of this is true?

Memories as Dispositions

Even though we know that the organization of the brain is made up
of a gazillion decision centres,
that neural activities going on at
one level of organization are inex-
plicable at another level, and that
as with the Internet, there seems
to be no boss, the puzzle for humans remains. The lingering conviction that we humans have a
"self" making all the decisions
about our actions is not
dampened. It is a powerful and
overwhelming illusion that is almost impossible to shake.[3] [4]
- Michael Gazzaniga

If we consider the notion of memories and
mental images as non-physical entities located
in private "spaces", puzzling questions arise.
Do memories and images exist *un-had:* i.e., do
they exist outside of conscious episodes? Can

---

3   Gazzaniga, Michael S., Who's in Charge?: Free Will
    and the Science of the Brain, Harper Collins: Kindle
    Edition (2011-11-15) p. 75.
4   The past forty years of research have shown that the
    human brain has billions of neurons organized into
    local, specialized circuits for specific functions,
    known as modules. For instance, in the human brain,
    an example of different circuits running in parallel
    and processing different inputs was demonstrated by a
    neuroimaging study done by Mark Raichle, Steve
    Petersen, and Mike Posner. One part of the brain
    reacts when you hear words, another particular part of
    the brain reacts to seeing words, still another area
    reacts while speaking words, and they can all be going
    at the same time.
    See also: Gazzaniga, Michael S., Who's in Charge?:
    Free Will and the Science of the Brain. Harper
    Collins: Kindle Edition (2011-11-15) p. 33.

two persons experience identical images? Do images have "rear" surfaces which are not being experienced? What are images made of? What is the connection between the space images seem to occupy and real space? Are there laws for private space?

The notion that memories are autonomous dispositional events dissolves such questions. Our understandings of cognitive proceedings are unaffected by the possibility that memories are not stored but created as required. Just as we are said to have reflexes, habits, conditioned responses, dispositions to act ... without thinking that they exist in particular locations, dispositions to have "memory-experiences" need not have cognitive addresses.

For the same reason we rarely ask: "Where is a stream of water located?", memories do not exist until evoked. Memories emerge in step-wise fashion, each step achieved by conditioned-response networks, multiplied, multiplexed and gated in complex ways.

A benefit of this explanation is that any number of memories can arise from finite sets of elements. Memory-experiences involve associations, with individual 'components' available to be reused endlessly. Thus, a body of water can form into new waves endlessly.

This explanation accomplishes another feature the realist view has difficulty with. Memories are not snapshots coming rapidly enough to give the illusion of continuity. Memories flow because they are laid down by flowing experiences.

A further difficulty involves the storing of representations. How could any top-down or outside-in program accomplish this? In addition, a constant (presumably increasing) expenditure of energy would seem necessary to maintain stored representations.

These difficulties are eliminated if memories are understood as being generated as required. Memories occur the way water rushes down channels scored by 'original' rains; recreating patterns again and again. This model easily scales up to explain the way cultural resources permeate lives, and perhaps even why wars grind and obliterate lives, until they have run their course.

On the dispositional model, memories and conscious episodes are triggered by local events, conversations, dreams or internal ruminations. When courses have been run, memories accomplish their own concluding— another requirement traditional accounts struggle with.

In the dispositional model, memories are storms that rise up, even if they only amount to tempests in tea pots. They rise up and fade away on their own recognizance.

The common sense/realist model has other difficulties. Would memories be 'replaced' at original addresses when individuals are finished using them? Or are memories copied from templates that remain in place? If they are not, what keeps memory stalls available until cognitive proceedings conclude and are done with them?

The notion of consciousness as efficacious does not explain any of these difficulties for the same reason talking about God explains nothing. We are enamoured with the idea that consciousness does stuff because we think of ourselves as little Gods creating choices out of nothing but acts of will.

This would be a relatively harmlessly conceit, but most human beings go good deal further. We believe we are in communication with the Divine, and believe that God has something

SAVE THE WORLD

special in mind for faithful fans.

In the 17th century, Descartes—the father of modern philosophy—thought that the pineal gland was the locus of interaction between the spiritual and the corporeal world. Although Descartes' choice has been caricatured, I think we all harbour an identical fantasy: consciousness is the locus of interaction between human agency and the rest of creation.

Self-enabling Dispositions

An important advantage of regarding memories as self-enabling dispositions involves the way the model explains experience. There is no need for additional cognitive functions to account for the spontaneous characteristic of subjective lives and conscious episodes.

The explanation illuminates our ability to see figures in ambiguous shapes—including dreadful creatures lurking behind bushes and along fence lines. As well, the notion of self-enabling dispositions explains tropes. Tropes are often found in psychology textbooks. They feature ambiguous figure-ground images that switch before our eyes; or images that emerge out of ambiguous stimuli: Rorschach ink blot responses, faces in clouds, the man in the moon ...

As well as being interesting, tropes provide a way of thinking about the belief that emerges when we are children. We all become subjects of experience. Things and ideas happen to us. We see ourselves as beings that exist outside of, or deep inside, what is going on.

This belief, combined with capacious memories, generates the points of view 'before our eyes' expressions refer to. Meaning occurs when further proceedings distill or reify (promote to 'thing' status) objects, entities and events from patterns in experience.

SAVE THE WORLD

According to commonsense and realism, these objects and entities exist in an external world and are perceived because we have eyes to see. Quasi-objects such as hurricanes, tornadoes or storms are referred to metaphorically, and so we say "The tornado touched down." or "The storm is over."

According to realists, the inner worlds of individuals more or less adequately reflect what is going on externally. Responses to events are compiled, adjudicated and controlled by conscious faculties. This is why, when persons are asleep or drugged, they are regarded as incapable of choosing or controlling themselves and therefore cannot be praised or blamed for what they get up to.

In the alternative sketched here, this sequence is turned on its head. Image-laden experiences occur. Each person distills an imaginary landscape out of these experiences and divides the results into *inner* and *outer* portions. Each person sees himself or herself as the point of view at the centre of this inner realm, and simultaneously as travelling across an actual, outer world in a body she possesses and controls.

The fact that real events subsidize fantasies in useful ways does not mean they are true. There are no corresponding artifacts 'out there', no perfect horses or trees in Platonic Realms, no noumenal horses or trees as Immanuel Kant proposed.

Put another way, there is no division between *inner* and *outer*—no matter how useful this partitioning may be. There are no partitions between you and me either. We are more like waves that appear to be approaching one another or the shore. The simpler story is that the wind generating our lovely waves may be favourable for the moment. We seem to be going our separate, merry ways, but will soon wind up, fantasies collapsing back into the events they were distilled out of.

In the meantime, we catch glimpses of what is going on. Watching squirrels and birds ... wild animals in general, is like being in a glass-bottom boat. You and I are vantage points. The advantage vantage points make possible is that we can become note-taking, note-comparing beings. This means we get to wistfully watch other creatures going about their lives naturally and spontaneously, without pesky conscious episodes getting in their way and tripping them up.

A further glimpse into what is going on occurs when figure-ground relationships reverse. If these reversals happen too rapidly to serve any purpose, chicken/egg or egg/chicken ... events expand until nodes can be identified and perhaps named. This is how chicken or eggs first questions come into existence.

Not only do we catch only occasional glimpses of what is going on, we have no idea what these glimpses look like to one another. Subjective lives consist of irreducibly private insights.[5] Realists acknowledge epistemological difficulties between what we think is true and what is actually occurring. On this understanding, the task of truth seekers, scientists and persons of good will is to bring these elements as close together as possible.

The problem is, the task cannot be completed and we have no (non-utilitarian) way of judging whether any step is right or wrong. The truth is, the truth is neither out there nor within us. As "chicken or egg first" questions warn, there is no truth of the matter because

---

5   Ludwig Wittgenstein talked about experiences as
     analogous to possessing a beetle in a matchbox that
     we cannot show to anyone, only describe.

there is no matter to speak of.

All that can be said is that something is going on. The things that make up this *something* are culturally-honed predictions about what will happen next. Therefore, the world and the world's elements and entities, are best guesses—not of what is *out there,* but of what will happen next.

The Single Memory Myth

A useful experiment can be performed from the comfort of your chair.

I propose that it is impossible to form an image of any object or entity, be it leaf, bumble-bee or rock, without seeing that object in the context of a tree, a flower or the ground.

If an object is extracted from any recognizable context, it must still be viewed within a nimbus of awareness that depends upon the person having previously acquired object-relevant *meaning* in context-rich circumstances.

For identical reasons, the notion of a (single) memory, laid down as a discrete entity which could be recalled, remembered, apprehended, and then restored to a database of memories, is incoherent.

In subjective lives, perceptions and experiences keep rolling and including more and more of what is going on. Habituation, peripheral vision, peripheral hearing ... dismiss events after safe intervals clearing a space for new conscious episodes.

As a result, subjective lives seem continuous. Memories elicit and evoke one another automatically, generating conscious episodes or dreams depending upon the time of day, the quality of companions and (a new factor) whether smart phones are available. This spontaneity reflects the flowing nature of original experiences. The sense of permanence the world seems to possess reflects the reliable ways cultural assets and disposition-based memories evoke and invoke one another.

In short, the mechanics of subjective life experiences present no difficulty for the notion of memories as micro-dispositions. We automatically, spontaneously, seamlessly ... remember ourselves, the world and people we have experienced. These recollections occur without conscious initiation or supervision. This may be all that needs to be said. Networks of concatenating dispositional elements are invoking one another and occasionally generating conscious episodes. These episodes stitch together into seamless notions of selves, objects and an actual world.[6]

The cognitive resources of human beings are sufficiently capacious that we sometimes experience ourselves experiencing. When this occurs in a context wherein individuals have been named and encouraged to think of themselves as persons, we almost always come to understand ourselves as 3-dimensional (spatial) entities enduring across time. The success of science is taken as further proof that the world exists independently of us, and that we are increasingly sophisticated about how it works.

The simpler story is that we do not 'live in' the world—even if 'live in' is understood in Heraclitus' "cannot step in same river twice" terms.

Each human being has a separate sense of the world and what is going on in it. We compare notes, make predictions and sometimes collaborate on projects based on these predictions. When things are going well, this is because we are all busy repairing and paddling the dreamboat we think into existence and that seems to be keeping us afloat.

---

6   These proceedings are relentless. The brain is constantly being rewired. http://www.thestar.com/news/world/2014/04/07/how_ the_internet_may_be_changing_the_way_we_read.

String Theory

Persons who claim that human beings make conscious choices typically think that this is nothing more than common sense and that nothing more needs to be said. To be sure, choices sometimes fail to be executed, but this is always because something got in the way. As well, persons often change their minds, using free will, a second or third time.

Unless something like this happens, 'choices' remain accomplishments of the persons whose choices they are. Even being countermanded does not alter the fact that a choice existed for a time. In other words, every choice becomes an eternal fact! This is sometimes spoken of in Christian terms. As an angel and an almost perfect being, Satan's choice to set up a dark kingdom in opposition to God cannot be undone—even if Satan were to wish it so!

In fact, Satan cannot wish it so because of his perfect nature. As a consequence, Satan must continue doing all he can to obstruct God's hope for human beings.

Because we make similar claims, you and I are in a similar predicament. We see ourselves as exceptional creatures generating choices right and left. Indeed, given that human beings now number seven billion, each making hundreds if not thousands of choices every day, the number of eternal facts being generated defies comprehension.

In spite of this profusion, in spite of the fact that even challenged human beings make choices from an early age, we insist that no other creature has this capability—although we acknowledge that choice-capable beings may exist elsewhere in the universe.

The consequences of this remarkable arrogance lie all around us, and nowhere more clearly than in the way we regard other creatures. Human beings harvest other forms of life for any purpose whatsoever: making them into pets, beasts of burden or consuming them directly.

As long as 'undue cruelty' is avoided, these practices are morally acceptable. We claim this prerogative because we believe other forms of life are incapable of making choices. The logic is straightforward. Unable to choose to not be harvested, farmed or 'petrified' ... they have no relevant feelings or thoughts, no terrors, no feelings of boredom or repugnance. Nothing that happens to them counts as a moral issue.

Thus, if even one human being 'pardons' and rescues one turkey at Thanksgiving, the super-erogatory quality of human beings' morality is underscored.

The ' capacity to feel, and to know that one is-feeling, is a critical component of cultural events. This is why CBC Radio's Anna-Marie Tremonte (a brusque, take-no-prisoners wo-man) spends so much time examining her guests' emotional responses to events, and scarcely any time investigating why these events occurred or what other consequences might be in play.

We think the capacity to feel—and the con-sciousness required to know that one is feeling—sets human beings apart from other creatures. This is why grief counsellors rush to children whose classmates have been murdered by megalomaniacs, committed sui-cide or gotten themselves run over while tex-ting.

The claim that only human beings have feel-ings defines and sanctions our exceptionalism. Worms wriggling on hooks, embryos terminated before the end of the second trimester, animals in factory farms ... are discounted according to this logic. People with unusual skin colour, cultural practices or sexual orientation are at risk because of this logic.

The implicit argument is that the capacity to have feelings implies a consciousness deep enough to contain a sense of self, personal history and destiny. "If you're happy and you know it clap your hands!" sets the stage for talk about persons, agency, choices and culpability. Ironically, it has also been diminishing the likelihood that we will have much to clap about—audiences, sports fans and Kim Jong-un's terrified acolytes notwithstanding.

In the following, I suggest why cultural practices involving hand-clapping, hand-waving and finger-pointing are based on a false premise and sketch an understanding that could be put in its place.

If we think about what must be involved putting choices into play, it is obvious that more is needed than awareness of a desirable or fearful outcome. 'Eternal fact' status notwithstanding, choices must be pushed into the world if they are to count—or even be noticed by anyone other than their author. This is true whether the world is thought of as a seamless event (my preference) or as a thicket of objects, entities and causes bringing objects and entities into and out of existence.

What would such pushing consist of? To gain a sense of this, it is useful to compare choices and strings. Choices have logical connections with individuals whose choices they are. Strings can be thought of in the same way. Like strings, choices do not have sufficient rigidity to make headway. As soon as we imagine them extended beyond the beings whose choices they are, 'outside events' begin participating in what is occurring.

In other words, whether thought of as the free will achievements of incarnated souls or the fruits of physiological and psychological proceedings, choices only have traction within beings giving rise to them.

We walk, talk, move our arms ... according to various desires rising from unconscious internal events, or because of unconscious internally-mediated responses to external events. Thinking about this in string terms is instructive. Strings cannot be pushed. On the other hand, a grapple on a rope (a big string!) allows me to haul a stick close enough to get my hands on it and transform it into a 'corporeal extension'. This extends my arm and the sphere wherein 'my choices' can have consequences. 'My choices' now range over a wider terrain. My sense of being a choosing person is enlarged!

In similar ways, a musician's instrument becomes an extension of his or her being, as does a backhoe in expert hands. The intentions of musicians and backhoe operators extend through their instruments.

Now comes the exciting part! These instruments, these extensions ... become factors and elements generating choices. Anyone in possession of a new tool invariably finds themselves 'inventing' and 'choosing' projects the new tool makes possible or more readily accomplished.

Learning a new word or concept similarly enlarges the scope of possible choices.

In other words, 'person choosing' is a figure of speech referring to the present state of an always changing set of resources and experiences. These assets anthropomorphize into free will talk and sanction ever-larger spheres of claimed sovereignty. Moon mining and Mars colonies are already on drafting tables. As far as I know, Kim Jong-un and Donald Trump do not have extraterrestrial ambitions but these are early days!

This process works the other way as well. As we age and decline, 'choice spheres' (notions of what is possible) shrink. This is a blessing. It would be terrible to be locked in an old body harbouring doomed youthful choices.

What is important to note is that choices reflect what is intrinsically possible at various stages of our lives. This sense of possibility can be extended with sticks, back-hoes, violins and—to take a modern example—deep-ocean drilling rigs and nuclear weapons.

If choices do not emanate from God-given souls or evolutionary achievement but from the number and potency of tools, then what we get up to is always a function of what we have been getting up to. This means there is nothing saying no to ambitions and projects except brutal Malthusian conclusions.

The only repair possible is a way of understanding ourselves that opposes the arrogance —and existential terrors—self-aware beings are prone to.

With this in mind, I offer another reason why the notion of 'persons choosing' is incoherent. Logically, everything persons are aware of is stale-dated. There are many reasons for this. The most important is that an event must have occurred, or at least gotten underway, before awareness is possible. In addition, information requires time to travel, and still more time to be processed into contents of awareness. More than eight minutes is required for light to travel to the earth from the sun. During this interval, human beings cannot know whether the sun has winked out or gone nova.

SAVE THE WORLD

Similarly, if you and I are three meters or three kilometres apart, our awareness of one another proportionately lags the events constituting our being. You may object that the intervals are so small that they can be ignored. (Albert Einstein handled this by speaking of local simultaneity.) However, no matter how small, intervals matter when thinking about what can sensibly be said about intentions and choices.

Each of us imagines a world with ourselves at its centre, full of human beings, creatures and cultural expectations. These images reflect efforts to anticipate what will happen based on news that is always more or less out-of-date.

Based on this belated information, a stream of premonitions, expectations and predictions occur. Within constraints imposed by bodies, sometimes extended with sticks, violins and backhoes, responses occur.

I see a rabbit. I throw a rock towards where I expect the rabbit to be when the rock gets there.

This is a far cry from the story we have been telling ourselves about magisterial human beings with an almost Divine capacity to understand, choose and act.

What would be gained if we discarded the conceit that consciousness makes choices and can act upon its own contents? An important benefit would be the realization that the capacity to see ourselves, and see ourselves inhabiting an imaginary world, is all that separates us from other forms of life.

Euler's Identity and Realism

$$e^{i\pi}+1=0$$

Euler's identity is regarded as one of the most beautiful mathematical equations ever achieved.

According to Prof David Percy from the Institute of Mathematics and its Applications (http://www.ima.org.uk/):

> ... "It is simple to look at and yet incredibly profound, it comprises the five most important mathematical constants—zero (additive identity), one (multiplicative identity), e and pi (the two most common transcendental numbers) and i (fundamental imaginary number)."

> "It also comprises the three most basic arithmetic operations—addition, multiplication and exponentiation".

> "Given that e, pi and i are incredibly complicated and seemingly unrelated numbers, it is amazing that they are linked by this concise formula."

If, a process model eventually replaces realism —the notion of objects and entities in a presently-existing material world—objects and entities will be understood as reifications, gestalts, images ... concocted by human beings (and other creatures) for reasons involving computational efficiency and success.

You ask: success for or as what? We will then be talking about narratives featuring reliably enduring, coherent processes; the way we now talk about clouds that sometimes look like monsters or people and sometimes spawn hurricanes warranting attention and names 'of their own'.

SAVE THE WORLD

As realists, we believe that object and entities exist separately from one another. They come into (and pass out of) existence by way of midwifery processes: stellar and organic evolution, conception, birth, death ...

If realism turns out not to be true, realizations should already be occurring on the front lines of research and understanding.

I think this is the case. For almost a century physicists have been talking about cosmologies featuring relativity and quantum physics.

Albert Einstein sidestepped the realism vs. process cosmology issue by talking about *local simultaneity* - exceptions to the special and general theories of relativity that allowed Newtonian physics to apply wherever awarenesses occur but nowhere that awarenesses had not yet seized upon and *realized*.

This was the issue Alfred North Whitehead took exception to. The cosmology in his book *Process and Reality* approached the question of being from the bottom up rather than from the top down or outside in.

It is interesting to think about mathematics in such terms. My understanding is rudimentary so what follows is mere conjecture.

Here is the identity again:

$$e^{i\pi}+1=0$$

What is needed is a definition of terms:

> *e* represents the natural logarithm of continuous growth and is irrational (cannot be expressed as a fraction).
>
> *i* represents the imaginary number ob-

tained by taking the square root of -1. This is also the number obtained by taking a derivative, i.e., the slope of a tangent to any curved surface. Although derivatives are approximated in practical situations with non-imaginary numbers, if the process was taken to its conclusion (i.e., to infinity) *i* would result.

π is the irrational number obtained by dividing the diameter into the circumference of any circle.

What does this have to do with realism? On the standard view, numbers were invented when human beings devised ways to count recurring objects and entities.

The assumption has always been that these were *found objects* but a simpler explanation is possible. Counting strategies could have emerged to keep track of the imaginary objects human beings were comparing and contrasting, imaginary objects distilled by cognitive processes yielding *reifications, gestalts* or *images.*

From the point of view of individual beings, nothing changes. The difference involves the status of things. There are no actual things in a presently existing material world—there are only approximations, derivatives, predictions, expectations ...

Since we are talking about imaginary objects and entities distilled out of recurring events—for example, discussing the location of stones in a stream so community members can cross without getting wet—the fact that human beings invented numbers is a poor basis for realist claims.

It is said that we use base 10 numbers because this is how many fingers we have.

SAVE THE WORLD

Arithmetic systems did not have 0 until someone thought about subtracting 1 from 1. The notion of negative numbers soon followed. Then—by performing addition, subtraction, multiplication and division upon the results— the *real number line* swam into view; a veritable zoo of possibilities with, for example, an infinite set of numbers between 0 and 1 as well as infinite sets of odd and even numbers.

What does this mean? I suggest that when human beings began distilling notions of objects out of 'object-free reality', we imported something of reality's flowing nature, along with the apparently countable results underwriting realism and common sense.

Thus, even though we can add, subtract multiply and divide numbers, we sometimes come up with rational results and sometimes not, as is the case with the symbols in Euler's identity.

It is these pesky irrational, imaginary, transcendental ... numbers that could be blowing the whistle on what we are up to. These numbers share 'DNA evidence' of their genesis as approximations, as crude partitions imposed upon what is going on. You and I have reasons for doing what we do, but these reasons are far removed from the undivided nature of what is going on.

If we look at Euler's identity, all the interesting stuff is occurring in the first term. The elements are either irrational or imaginary. The identity tells us that if we take the results of this computation and add 1 the result is: 0. Interestingly, the same result occurs if **e$i\pi$** is replaced with **-1**.

What could this signify? The thing that occurs to me is that the number 1 could be thought of as a consequence of fishing information from the stream of being, fashioning the distilled results into phenomenal objects and then

HOW PHILOSOPHY COULD

discovering that these images could be tallied up, added and subtracted in sophisticated ways.

Presumably **-1** represents undoing this mischief.

Euler's identity could be telling us that realism-based arithmetic does not withstand scrutiny.

Einstein's Brain[7]

> ... the voices of the dead
> will utter me forever.
> - Jorge Luis Borges

> I'm inclined to think we are all
> ghosts—every one of us.
> - Henrik Ibsen

> For us believing physicists, the
> distinction between past, present
> and future is only an illusion, even
> if a stubborn one.
> - Albert Einstein

Albert Einstein's brain resides in a Tupperware container somewhere on Planet Earth.

A portion has been subjected to histological analysis. A 1985 paper in *Experimental Neurology* suggested that the brain was endowed with an unusual profusion of glial cells in the left hemisphere thought to be the seat of mathematical and language abilities.

The suggestion is that this may have contributed to Einstein's accomplishments.

We are attracted to such findings because we hope they might lead to injectable solutions enhancing creativity and subjective life.

At the same time, such inquiries raise provocative questions. When we applaud Albert Einstein ... are we applauding the person or his neural anatomy? If 'Einstein the person' is only the initial consciousness benefiting from some physiological wellspring, the most the world owes him is gratitude for

---

7   A version of this piece appears on:
    www.backlander.ca

sharing.

Indeed, the public could be thought to share in the honour, since some of us had enough sense to dialogue with Einstein's neural substrate and facilitate his genius.

In other words, Einstein the conscious person was arguably no more involved in his achievements than people in his life, insofar as his neural substrate was the engine of creativity.

Of course, ruminations and reflections that occurred during these conscious episodes were important. Einstein shared many of these episodes in his writings and reminiscences.

This does not eliminate the underlying question. If a fortuitous neural endowment was responsible for Einstein's productions, then lesser substrates in people like you and I also participated as cultural resources, in the guise of friends, fellow students, critics and parochial interests.

Where does this leave us? There is a tension between speaking of persons as moral and intellectual agents and curiosity about organic and cultural precursors of what people get up to. At the end of this investigation we might not be able to give *Einstein the person* credit for anything at all. The notion of 'person' will become a banal, 3-dimensional way of referring to human beings at vanishingly small points in time.

In this prospect, there are no persons possessing feet, eyes or brains ... Persons are what happens when neural substrates (along with the other bits and pieces comprising bodies) are embedded in physical and cultural circumstances. Persons are like sounds emanating from radios tuned to particular frequencies.

SAVE THE WORLD

If we take this argument *inside*—if we consider the sense we each have of being alive in the world—it is not clear why episodes of self awareness support claims that the subjects of these awarenesses are therefore authors of thoughts, owners of bodies pr inventors of theories.

Nor does the fact that awarenesses occasionally participate in subsequent events, however seductive and important the connections. Blackboards have nothing to do with equations or prose, even if they could not have occurred without blackboards' 'computational assistance'.

In short, the Einstein person was no more involved in his creative output than others in his life—except, of course, that it was his 'neural substrate' melding internal and external events and generating *insights*.

Thinking thus, we have good reason to be interested in the machinery generating insights. Thomas Harvey was correct to 'rescue' Einstein's brain, since cognitive life is reputed to centre in the cranium. The problem is, reductionist arguments rarely stop where they should. Harvey may have inadvertently discarded parts of Mr. Einstein as essential as his cortex. Such zest, after all, must have had hormonal elements. Perhaps an unusual neural substrate coupled with unusual levels of testosterone was involved ... a possibility Einstein's documented fascination with women sanctions.

Part of the problem is that we are not in the habit of valuing whole beings. Instead, we localize creativity and consciousness within bodies because we wish to encapsulate the essence of person-hood. If persons consisted of bodies to the last cell, we would lose much of the rationale for speaking of them as owners or agents. The strategy has been to deny physiological and neural substrates agent status. Beyond primitive 'supporting roles', anatomical characteristics are not linked with the mental events moral and spiritual claims depend upon. Instead of being the ground of awareness, the body is a 'vehicle' piloted by the person whose vehicle it is.

This is the stuff of common sense and ordinary conversation. Einstein gets the credit and not some neural substrate. More importantly, we get to speak of souls surviving death, of transmigration, reward and punishment.

There are puzzles of course. If nothing about physical being is causally linked to behaviour, at least behaviour that is of interest to moralists, it is hard to understand why particular 'organic vehicles' should be punished or feted, imprisoned or provided with luxurious lives. If agency talk is as meaningful as 'Order of Canada' medals have it, good or bad behaviour has no *sine qua non* connection with bodies or histories. Consistent observers could only announce that something wonderful (or terrible) had occurred. They could advise that this event happened near this or that assemblage of skin, hair and teeth; and that this might be a good place to hang around (or avoid).

We seem to have two options.

1. We can continue looking for neural substrates and run the risk of not having any unpredictable behaviour. (The only interesting reason for speaking of persons is the belief that actions transcend determinism and cannot be anticipated.)

2. We can continue to believe that there is more to us than meets the eye—no matter how omniscient or penetrating eyes become.

To the extent that we are interested in brains in Tupperware containers, (2) is undermined. Sooner or later, we may be reduced to speaking of excellence in the way we presently speak of Rolls Royce automobiles, software packages and profitable corporations.

— 2 —

The possibility that persons might not be sources of human conduct, that important causal chains have 'external world' origins, raises important questions. Would human beings be morally paralyzed if 'actions' turn out to have sufficient non-conscious choice antecedents and become *behaviours*? Even if we cannot presently always say what they consist of, we have invested heavily in the assumption that such explanations are available.

I think this means 'extenuating circumstances' will eventually be seen as totalling to 100%. On the present model of morality and responsibility, this would contradict moralizing's principal activity ... prescribing punishments to balance the moral equation: "An eye for an eye ..."

Some of this spade work has already been done. For at least a century, western cultures have been integrating moralizing talk with behaviouristic explanations. These efforts proceed case by case, establishing precedents which are then used to mete out punishments in tempered ways.

Unhappily, this incremental approach seems shallow and unsavoury. The issue of whether moral talk will eventually have to be abandoned or rethought is never acknowledged. Even though tacit recognition exists, there is at least one elephant in courtrooms no one is honestly talking about.

We talk instead about extenuating circumstances and gravely discuss dictums such as "ought implies can". The resulting distinctions between 'degrees' of murder and manslaughter, for example, are having far-reaching consequences. Pre-sentencing investigations evaluate habitual criminality, traumatic childhood experiences, physiological conditions ... to assess rehabilitation possibilities and security risks.

This is well and good, but fails to confront the underlying issue. We claim that functional human beings: those spared deforming experiences, those not in the grip of passion ..., are more accountable than those who are not. At the same time, we praise and reward useful, creative behaviour without making parallel distinctions. The financially advantaged and intellectually gifted are applauded for artistic or scientific accomplishments as vigorously if they had struggled through adversity every step of the way.

In short, a moral, legal and intellectual crisis lurks in the tension between praising and blaming on one hand and attempting to account for behaviour on the other. Behaviourists avoid this dilemma by focusing upon particular actions. There is always enough complex 'human stuff' going on outside of what is being investigated that alarm bells do not go off.

This is why Dr. Harvey's project is portentous: if connections can be drawn between physiological structures and extraordinary intellectual accomplishments, what person-hood means suddenly becomes unclear.

One thing is clear however. No redefinition of person-hood can require that human beings abandon rewarding and punishing. We may, however, have to be content with saying that circumstances require this or that rejoinder and leave off saying that person X deserves ... whatever we have in mind to mete out.

In this revised lexicon, individuals will continue to defend and promote themselves and one another in both ad hoc and principled ways. The good news is that better deterrence and more excellence may both be possible. A schedule of reinforcements and punishments uncontaminated by agent talk could have significant benefits.

On the other hand, giving up agent talk would also have consequences. Thinking of ourselves and one another as responsible agents has socializing and normative benefits. If we think we are accountable because we consciously author what we get up to, this may amount to an internal chamber of sober second thought and, in properly socialized individuals, *cause them to behave as if they were persons!*[8]

Again, these incremental, hesitant accommodations seem minute and unsatisfactory. If we stand back from what is going on it may be possible to frame persons differently. In an enlarged view, what we presently think of as 'persons' could become cross-sections of 4-dimensional space-time narratives. Indeed, this is the way the universe itself has been understood since Einstein (the putative owner of the brain under discussion) advanced the General Theory of Relativity (GTR).

---

8   To whit: Freud's superego and Christianity's *guardian angels.*

HOW PHILOSOPHY COULD

Not enough attention has been paid to the GTR's implications for notions of personality and morality. Persons continue to be regarded as 3-dimensional (spatially-extended) entities passing through time.

I think this has been having unfortunate consequences. Regarding oneself as a 3-dimensional entity encourages notions of personal invulnerability. Even behaviourists—who should know better—regard naturally natural aspects of organic being: personal space, skin, immune systems, directed attention, habituation ..., as defining and insulating individuals from 'outside' stuff'.

These boundaries are useful. They organize events so they can be counted. They help human beings think of themselves as entities. They parcel up what is going on into countable packages that can be named and owned. Boundaries are also key to notions of self-hood and notions of agency. Commonsense and realism become *self-evident* because packages are thought of as existing in this or that place. We are not surprised that creatures can move around, chase down possibilities and get out of harm's way. Boundaries, partitions, skins ... encourage the notion that human beings can 'get away' with stuff at least some of the time, and that it makes sense to try to do so.

As soon as persons think of themselves in 4-dimensional terms, as soon as they see conscious episodes as 3-dimensional slices of 4-dimensional narratives, such notions are re-framed as nodes or sub-events of larger events. Neural, physiological and cultural events can now become part of conversations about the best way to maximize the wholesomeness and vitality of subjective lives because all are seen as having a common source.

50

SAVE THE WORLD

This 3-dimensional standpoint makes it easy to slip between behaviouristic and agent talk depending upon the needs of the moment. Concern for communities and the biosphere would improve if 'individuals' understood that their being is rooted in the past anticipates the future, and that their 'spatial boundaries' are not as well-defined as skins imply.

Einstein's Special Theory of Relativity introduced local simultaneity as a way of accommodating commonsense notions. In the commonsense Newtonian universe, a 3-dimensional plane exists across the universe, with every region advancing simultaneously through time. The General Theory of Relativity made it meaningless to speak of space and time separately.

I think this means persons can no longer be considered spatially-extended (3-dimensional) entities passing through time. Whatever existence means, it seems clear that entities require simultaneous spatial and temporal extension. It follows that entities cannot have a second helping of duration ... as the idea of passing through time requires.

For our purposes, this means persons cannot have supervisory relationships with the events comprising their existence. (Einstein bundled such issues under 'local simultaneity' and hurried on to more important problems.)

As well, spatially-distributed entities do not exist at any 'point in time'. The distribution of extended bodies, and the time required to communicate from one side to another, does not matter for all intents and purposes ... save for the notion of intents and purposes.

It is significant that the expression *human being* can be replaced with *human event* with no loss of meaning. In addition, since human beings are not always wilful (i.e., when sleeping or indifferent), occasionally emerging conscious volitions would have to neutralize or integrate with existing processes preparatory to heading them in some direction. These 'entry points' would have to be spatio-temporally extended as well, to link up with external processes preparatory to giving them a judicious twist.

Finally, for the idea of conscious choice to make sense, there must be things human beings get up to that could not be explained any other way. The Law of Parsimony or Occam's Razor states that the simplest explanation is almost always the best explanation.

In addition, the evolution of consciousness and conscious choice machinery would have to be explained, a notoriously difficult undertaking. Moreover, it would have to be explained in a way that restricts its presence to just human beings.

Even if these difficulties are ignored, choices still have to be put into play in ways that 'volition receptors' and motor neurons received suitably orchestrated inputs. With Einstein's help, we understand that (non-quantum) communications proceed at finite speed. This constraint places an additional computational burden upon hypothetical agents.

I am not aware of such efforts nor have I heard others speak of them. And if I am not conscious of such efforts, and therefore not consciously invoking them, what would such proceedings have to do with the agency claims human beings have been making?

There is a way to sidestep these issues. We can re-frame persons so that they are thought of as spatially and temporally extended events. In this story, we cannot talk about a person until his or her narrative is concluded—i.e., until he or she is dead. Only then is it possible to say: "That's Tom".

In the meantime, "That's Tom so far" is all we can say. I think this means that it is a mistake to identify Tom with any of the processes constituting the Tom event, or any glimpses people have of Tom along the way.

This also illuminates why it is hard to understand how 3-dimensional manifestations could be responsible for 4-dimensional narratives. Such talk is analogous to saying stages of a storm are responsible for subsequent stages just because each is a conduit through which the storm passes.

There are, of course, plenty of reasons to evaluate complex events: take temperatures, consult barometers, conduct political polls ... These benefits have nothing to do with consciously evaluating findings and then issuing volitions. Conscious episodes sometimes occur when information combines with local events. The sight of geese flying south in the fall triggered interest in wood cutting in the community I grew up in. These episodes sometimes stimulated discussions and the felling of trees.

Now that most of us live in cities and our firewood is piped in from Alberta or some OPEC nation, the sight of geese flying south means something different or nothing at all.

The most important benefit of understanding persons in 4-dimensional terms is that this would diminish the habit of attaching good and bad outcomes to phantoms.

1. Villains and heroes would be seen as the present shape of underlyiing

events. They would be understood as having the reality of images in mirrors.

2. Fashioning such glimpses into scapegoats or heroes means opportunities to repair or promote proceedings at headwaters are wasted.

3. Scapegoats and heroes mean the events responsible for what is going on are not taken seriously or overlooked entirely.

There is another paralysis involved in scapegoating. As soon as I identify you as responsible for some state of affairs, there is nothing more to do except urge you to keep up the good work or make amends. You will be puzzled, and possibly annoyed, by my antics. If the issue is negative, you know that you are not consciously responsible for it because you are not consciously responsible for anything. You suspect that I am up to some mischief.

If I am praising you, you once again know that you have never done anything consciously. You conclude that I am an idiot, up to something or you take the money and run.

– 3—

What are we to make of rational and moral deliberations and actions taken to instantiate conclusions? From a 4-dimensional standpoint, persons are 3-dimensional phantasmagoria with no way of initiating volitions 'back into' what is going on. If rational and moral deliberations are so understood, acting becomes the responsibility of ghost-like conscious episodes stitched into a simulacrum of being.

This does not mean human beings cannot achieve intentional goals. The problem is that we think of ourselves as consciously conceiving thoughts and putting them into play. Since we also know that this is not true each of us thinks that he or she is fundamentally flawed. Everyone else seems to be a fully-functional moral and rational agent. In this circumstance the best strategy is to make no move that would attract attention. All that we are prepared to do is aggressively defend whatever it was that we found ourselves doing in the past. We know that we did not consciously orchestrate that either but if we are belligerent enough maybe we can get away with taking credit for it.

A simpler and I think more survivable story is that persons are constellations of inclinations, goals, and occasional conscious episodes. These conscious episodes function like blackboards. They help cognitive processes deepen insights and organize projects.

There is another reason besides facile belligerence that we have been able to sustain the fantasy that consciousness is efficacious. We are in the habit of diverting consciously-mediated proceedings into cultural cul de sacs, where discussions are understood as legitimate responses. When this sleight of hand is going well, insights and discussions are rarely thought of as interim stages of responses still to be undertaken. Instead of improving responses, thinking and talking lead to more thinking and talking. These proceedings can eliminate the need for responses indefinitely.

To be sure, sometimes a sound or a fury erupts. A cacophony of bellowing, gesticulating, clapping, marching, banging pots ... announces that something is going on.

Storms eventually subside. In these cases, the ensuing silence reassures participants and observers that something occurred, that a response has taken place. Everyone retires to their corner, marchers and pot-bangers content that they have done their part; onlookers reassured that the ramparts are manned and that nothing further will be required of them until another demonstration is called for.

In the meantime, problems continue metastasizing and villains continue chuckling their way to banks.

Here is how I think the notion of 3-dimensional persons became mankind's cultural engine. In primal circumstances, before languages and cultures emerged, individuals dealt with problems all the time. Solutions came to their minds and were instantly put into practice. Eventually, these individuals remembered that a series of problems, conscious episodes and responses had taken place. They noticed that they always seemed to at the centre of these proceedings. Why not take take the opportunity to claim that this awareness was conceiving and orchestrating solutions and responses?

Almost all of history has been infected by this fantasy. Human beings love to talk about realizations and insights, but only if they are *their* realizations and insights. Colleagues, peers, family members, citizens ... serve as sounding boards in these conscious prowess demonstrations.

Of course, a good deal more is going on. Although conversations are often fraught, individuals in communities cane exchange information and improve one another's sense of what should be done. These conversations also flesh out the world we seem to share. The idea of an external world, roughly corresponding to our imaginations and conversations, has been a cultural *fait accompli* for thousands of years. There is even a venerable branch of philosophy called *epistemology* worrying about the reliability of information human beings glean from the external world, or whether any information can be trusted.

There is no need to worry. We cannot get the external world wrong. The world is whatever human beings collectively imagine it to be.

Perhaps ten thousand years ago, populations had grown sufficiently and human activities had become complicated enough that industrial-strength solutions became possible. The results included nations, governments and corporations. Small at first, these organizations became an invasive species and, a few hundred years ago, began co-opting and enveloping everything.

Along the way, moral, intellectual and pragmatic concerns became the responsibility of academics, priests, politicians and professionals. The resulting focused competencies discouraged 'amateurs', whose efforts have always seemed primitive in comparison. The paradox is that, as the problems and solutions professionals pose and solve grow larger and more sophisticated, what is going on is increasingly ignored by professionals and everyone else.

As well, as cultures become sophisticated, individuals are correspondingly marginalized in moral and rational terms. In the face of specialized expertise and stupendous problems, what can anyone say that has not already been said better?

To be sure, academics and big-picture thinkers regularly encourage populations to improve their moral and rational understandings. They seem unaware of their historical contribution to widespread indifference or apathy. Indeed, these contributions have been baked into economic and cultural proceedings sufficiently that they can pontificate and promulgate to their hearts' content, content that their perches will remain secure. They soldier on in the face of apathy they are complicit in.

The second mischief deep thinkers are guilty of is that they assume that their understandings will be translated into action by less intellectually competent individuals.

I suggest that these are intellectual and moral Ponzi schemes. Moralizers and public intellectuals prosper in terms of money, prestige and feelings of accomplishment. Audiences and students are the new entrants needed to keep these pyramids inflated. Learned societies and professional journals record investigations into increasingly minute issues. Popularizers translate these otherwise inscrutable results sufficiently that the chattering classes glimpse how wonderful lives will be a year or ten down the road.

Big-picture thinkers divide human beings into *thinkers* and *doers.* Big Thinkers do all the research and heavy intellectual lifting. If the results can be translated into profitable enterprises, entrepreneurs and venture capitalists rush in. Self-driving vehicles, virtual reality, enhanced virtual reality, smart-phones with integrated pets and romantic partners ... what's not to like?

With such issues in the hands of a gifted minority, it is only fair that rest of us undertake the work we are capable of. We should pay taxes without whining. We should applaud at cultural events as often as possible. Al Gore's *An Inconvenient Truth* demonstrates how well this division of labour works. TED talks, documentary films, Noam Chomsky's indefatigable indictment of the USA as the world's premier state terrorist, David Suzuki's lecturing on environmental footprints ... share Mr. Gore's fatal premise. They all agree that it is possible to separate insights into problems from responses putting these insights into play. They all assume that centuries of this division of labour is not a factor in the fact that things are going to Hell in a hand basket.

The notion of consciousness as choice engine makes it seem plausible that human beings can pass insights around over the top of deterministic events. Since I may not have convinced you that the role of consciousness is less grandiose, I offer an argument that comes to the same conclusion without talking about consciousness at all.

To pass insights around with a view to having others act upon them requires that communications occur without loss of content or sense of urgency. I think this means communications must be digital and not analog. The difference between digital and analog is well-understood. Digital communications convey information reliably because 'noise on the line' is filtered out by the either/or nature of machine language: a switch is either on or off. An excellent example is the torrent of 0's and 1's powering the internet. Equally reliable and even more sophisticated communication is achieved with the 4 elements comprising DNA and RNA information. The other binary communication we know about asks the very important question: did you reproduce?

 All other organic communications are analog. Analog communications are subtle, nuanced, poetic, fraught with ambiguity and opportunities for misunderstanding. This is why languages are rich resources. However, this usefulness also challenges common notions of consciousness, agent-hood and responsibility. Agents require unequivocal information to make hard-edged decisions for which they can be held accountable. This is on the 'input' side. On the output side, whether responses occur with the help of conscious episodes or under the guidance of consciousness, responsibility requires assessing consequences actions before making decisions.

The problem is, there is no way to anticipate what will happen more than a few seconds or meters after responses occur. In other words, both in terms of information coming in or responses, 3-dimensional agents (conscious or otherwise) cannot be held responsible for what they get up to.

Even if human beings were able to accurately report ten minutes worth of consequences for God's *Book or Life* or to Homeland Security, these consequences would have been the result of responses conceived and acted upon without such information.

The other possibility is that people have expectations of good or bad results and that expectations are the moral issue. The difficulty is that this links morality with the capacity to make predictions. This does not seem to be something human beings consciously control.

With regards to information coming in,herrmeneutics worries about whether messages individuals, cultures and generations send are messages recipients receive. In Greek mythology, Zeus occasionally found it useful to send messages to human beings,despatching Hermes to get the job done. The problem is, even if Hermes received, remembered and enunciated messages perfectly, there was no way to test whether they had been understood as Zeus intended.

Even if Zeus had prepared digital transcriptions, there is no guarantee recipients' operating systems would deliver the correct conscious episodes.

Why does this matter? Al Gore demonstrated that the public rarely takes up the work Big Thinkers recommend. This is considered evidence of moral turpitude, apathy or, following Hillary Clinton, that one is deplorable. We now glimpse that the problem could be as simple as analog static on the line, or the semantic ambiguity analog communications more or less make inevitable.

Another possibility is that a sense of urgency has been lost. The only individuals that can be counted on to appreciate the need to get stuff done are the individuals having the insights.

The moral is that having ideas and talking about them is not the same as having ideas and acting upon them. if I act upon an insight, the conversation rate could be said to be 100%. If I have an insight and talk about it with a view to having someone else respond, the conversion rate usually drops to 0% .

Why have we travelled so far down this rocky road? There are several reasons: the ride has been exhilarating; people get to gossip; the rich seem to be getting richer and we all want to keep getting rich door open. However, I think the most important reason is that no one has to acknowledge responsibility for anything. Even individuals in jail or about to be executed are astonished at how things have turned out. It seems clear to all of us us that we are innocent. As far as we know, insights just keep flaring up. Sometimes we 'act upon them' but have no recollection of choosing to do so. This alchemy is not part of conscious episodes that occur while acting either. These episodes all involve achieving some result or avoiding disaster.

The icing on the insight/response layer cake is

that Big-Picture thinkers get to enjoy collegial respect, security, mutual stimulation, opportunities for arrogance and feelings of *noblesse oblige.* When their recommendations come to naught because no one is taking up the responsibility of responding feelings of moral and intellectual superiority are inevitable.

To the extent that human beings move from 3 to 4-dimensional notions, such distractions and temptations would diminish. Moral and intellectual insights would have a greater chance of being implemented. They would frequently become more robust. Nothing improves ideas faster than trying them out!

-- 4 --

If America is about nothing else, it is about the invention of the self. Because we have little use for history, because we refuse comforts based on the blueprint of class privilege, we find ourselves set adrift in an existential void, inheriting nothing save the obligation to construct a plausible self, to build a raft of identity.

- Lewis Lapham

On February 11, 1992, American heavyweight boxer Mike Tyson, a well-known contender for the world championship, was convicted of rape and sexually deviant conduct. He was expected to be sentenced to 6–10 years of incarceration. As Mr. Tyson was 25 years of age, this was thought to spell the end of his boxing career.

More than two decades have passed and we know more than we wanted to know about Mr.

Tyson's tribulations. Nonetheless, his life provides an opportunity to test the 4-dimensional model. Would there have been a different weighing of extenuating vs. internal determinants of conduct? Would Tyson's subjective life have sorted itself out the same way?

A two-panel cartoon circa 1992 captured the predicament. In the first panel, Tyson is enjoying the crowd's adulation after some boxing success. The caption trumpets: BESTIAL, MERCILESS, ANIMALISTIC. The second shows Mr. Tyson being led from the court in handcuffs. The caption is identical.

To his consternation and probably bewilderment, Tyson has been rewarded and punished for the same behaviour. The public does not want him 'behaving badly' outside of the ring, yet seems unaware of the tension between applauding and censuring identical behaviours.

To manage this problem, sports fans deploy a familiar defence. We applaud Tyson's boxing prowess because he is a person and should be given credit for consciously-orchestrated, gruelling achievements. By the same token, we condemn him for behaving badly when censure is warranted. How could Mr, Tyson object? He cannot expect 100% exculpation for 'bad behaviour' and still expect to be rewarded for prowess in the ring?

If these conflicting sanctions had not been baked into cultural activities so that they are starting points for what we get up to and think, sports fans would be left marvelling at the ways biological and circumstantial factors combine as behaviour. A few might worry about the loss of *persons acting* as an ontological category. A few more might consider the role of public adulation in the emergence of remarkable accomplishments and ugly behaviour.

I have no doubt that the status quo would survive. Abandoning 3-dimensional thinking would reduce the effectiveness of scapegoating. As well, if fans understood themselves as complicit in Tyson events, they would wince whenever icons behaved badly— although vicarious enjoyments and feelings of accomplishment would be on better ground.

The most important change is that populations no longer be able to deflect responsibility for what is going on by rewarding or punishing imaginary persons at the centre of achievements or transgressions. Moving to a 4-dimensional model would enlarge

- the scope and therefore the content of what is deemed admirable;
- the focus of remediation;
- the locus of nurturing.

The Tysons occupying the world's media and sometimes its judiciary are 3-dimensional manifestations of underlying events. Inasmuch as 4-dimensional understandings diffuse responsibility for what is going on across participants' narratives, Tyson manifestations would become focal points from which investigations begin.

These are deep waters however. To the extent that persons are understood in terms of genetic endowments and histories, we are unable to moralize about what they get up to as individuals situated at vanishingly small points of time. At the same time, the sphere of indictable events would expand because blame (and praise) must land somewhere. If responsibility cannot be attached to manifestations or apparitions, it must be apportioned across the elements generating them.

The result is that blaming and praising would

become more sensitive to the events spawning praiseworthy and blameworthy outcomes. Both cancers and cancerous individuals would still need to be identified and dealt with. By precluding scapegoating, 4-dimensional investigations mean we would more likely figure out why malignancies occur and do stuff to minimize them

----

Some progress has been made. In many nations, young offenders cannot be named. We recognize that children and adolescents are not responsible for what they get up to and should be shielded from social and career repercussions of bad behaviour. Unfortunately, this progress is occurring in the context of 3-dimensional notions and has been having unintended consequences. Not naming young offenders is based on the idea that they are unable to make appropriate cultural and prudential choices. However, the resulting unrequited responsibility has not been flowing through to relevant parents or communities. It vanishes. Important clues about what is wrong are being lost and timely repairs are not being made.

As social and economic circumstances worsen because timely repairs are not occurring, helicopter parenting has been running amok. Adolph Hitler's *Mein Kampf* is forbidden reading, along with Salinger's *Catcher in the Rye*, Margaret Laurence's *Stone Angel* and a growing list of once-innocuous titles.

Banned-book lists and other constraints upon young activities are occurring when interest in do-it-yourself entertainment is waning. Reading has become such an exotic activity that it is attaining magical status. A growing proportion of 1st worlders reads well enough to be advertised to, but not fluently enough to be able to reliably separate wheat from chaff.

HOW PHILOSOPHY COULD

This is causing consternation. If a word to the wise is sufficient, think of the harm treacherous books and politically incorrect talk could accomplish! Better safe than sorry!

On another front, if iconic public figures turn out to have been rascals, statues in their honour must be destroyed, official commendations rescinded.

In my understanding, leaving books on shelves and artifacts intact would be a better strategy. If intervention is deemed necessary, offensive artifacts could become teaching moments. Placing historical facts in context, in the form of footnotes and lists of consequences, would provide cautionary tales for future generations.

Scurrilous books should remain on shelves for the same reason. Sophisticated readers have no qualms about this. With lots of reading under their belts, every new book is ingested with a grain of salt. Surely young people should meet up with as many villains as possible in imaginary ways! There is no better way to become familiar with heroic and despicable people, immunize one's self against diseased thoughts and develop a cautionary sense of what human beings are capable of.

Our one-size-fits-everything axiom is that only persons (conscious, 3-dimensional manifestations of 4-dimensional events) are accountable. The problem is, this involves an impossibility—making sense of the notion that a person that exists right here and right now. The simpler story is that what we think of as persons are like calculus derivatives. They are, as Newton said, the ghosts of vanished quantities. They exist where distances along narrative curves become infinitely small. Derivatives are computationally important but no one believes they exist the way realism and morality propose that persons exist. The parallels are wonderful! Both are useful and both are imaginary. A inkling of what this means can be gained by asking a simple question: what is the duration of the present in the past-present-future model?

To return to the issue of helicopter parenting, wherever resources permit—which mostly means in 1st world nations—children and adolescents are shielded from the consequences of their own criminal behaviour and scandalous books. Materialism, instant gratification technologies ... mean that an alarming proportion of young people scarcely notice that they have been born. I do not think it an exaggeration to suggest that modern populations are being prevented from being born into 4-dimensional existence .

To be fair, these balances are hard to get right. The need to nurture and protect young people must be weighed against the need to moralize and scapegoat when things go badly. Thus, when youngsters get up to heinous conduct, they are sometime transferred to adult jurisdictions. Political correctness, sensitivity and empathy ... can only go so far! Deeply disturbing behaviour must be accounted for with censure and sanctions.

The alternative would be to let responsibility leach through to families and communities .

Has this been a good idea? Adolph Hitler, Saddam Hussein, Osama Bin Laden ... were malevolent presences, but they would have amounted to little more than caricatures had they not resonated with millions of similarly-disposed people. Because we are not in the habit of looking into the genesis of social upheavals, root causes continue to fester. Presently, President Donald Trump and Kim Jung-un are troubling the sleep of hundreds of millions of human beings. Remarkably, it is doubtful if any of these anxious individuals have any sense that they are complicit in what is going on. In the amazing modern world, we are all either innocent bystanders or aggrieved victims.

It does not have to be this way. There is no reason to worry that 4-dimensional understandings would prevent timely remedies because we would be unable to indict 3-dimensional ghosts. The comparison should be with cancer. We do not regard cancers as wilful entities. Cancers are as innocent as children and animals. This does not prevent them from being dealt with as soon as possible when doing so would save lives. We certainly do not hold cancers responsible for harms in order to continue practices styles contributing to their emergence.

Thus, holding tobacco corporations' feet to the fire perpetuated the praise/blame model that sanctioned advertising toxic substances in the first place. Corporations argued that they were innocent because customers were choosing whether to purchase. As far as I know, no one asked why corporations spent so much money advertising when, on their core defense, consuming decisions reflect conscious choices.

A case can be made that corporations were entitled to make product information available so consumers can make *informed choices.* This hardly describes modern commerce, which spent 750 billion dollars on advertising in 2016

What is it that we wish from each other? Is it to be left in peace? Is it to please and flatter one another? I think we should cajole, annoy and hector one another until we are forced off of our *present* perches and become fully-fledged 4-dimensional beings instead of 3-

dimensional phantoms. Ralph Waldo Emerson said it best:

> We are weary of lurking around corners, of gliding ghost-like through an increasingly slight and unreal world. We crave reality even if it comes in painful strokes. I (use this to) explain ... those excesses and errors of which souls of great vigor, but not equal insight, often fall. They feel the poverty at the bottom of all the seeming affluence of the world.

Emerson reminds us of another problem. Most cultures—certainly Christian and Islamic—propose that infants receive souls as a prerequisite to agent-hood. They agree that moral development is incremental and begins early on. Why then do families and communities—as soon as technology and resources permit—deny youngsters the benefits of sinewy experiences and outcomes? Do we really believe perpetual gratification is the road to maturity, responsibility and happiness? Do we believe being born was a mistake to be rectified as soon as technologies make external wombs possible?

On the other hand, no matter how indulged their childhood, we believe human beings transform into rational and moral agents as soon as they become adults.

Without 3-dimensional conceits and notions of incarnation, this would be as absurd in thought as it is in reality. Another dilemma confronts 3-dimensional morality. If we really believe human beings are moral and rational agents functioning freely at every moment, does this not preclude deterrence and rehabilitation issues from judicial proceedings? Should persons not be held accountable in the starkest sense—without taking extenuating circumstances into consideration? We are either moral agents or we are not. There are either no extenuating circumstances or they sum to 100%.

In other words, punishing and rewarding, and only punishing and rewarding, is consistent with 3-dimensional morality. Deterring bad and rewarding good behaviour is only permissible with children because they are not yet moral agents. Aristotle thought that the virtuous were effortlessly so. I think this means that Aristotle was a 4-dimensional moralist who framed morality in circumstances featuring human beings but not restricted to them.

There is another problem with the justice system. We cannot lay hold of the persons or agents needed to make the contraption fly. All we can deal with are completed acts. The person whose acts they are—the person whose 'decision' grounded them—is always an infinitesimal second beyond reach! The Tyson person the American judiciary laid hold of was not the person who 'committed' the crime.

Of course, there was a good chance that further Tyson manifestations would have unpleasant inclinations and pose similar threats, but this has nothing to do with morality from a 3-dimensional perspective.

Let me try to make this plausible. Individuals cannot be held responsible for doing something until an act has occurred. Once committed, acts move from imaginary or hypothetical to 4-dimensional reality. From a 3-dimensional standpoint, long rap sheets or sparkling resumes are equally irrelevant. As soon as acts occur, moral questions dissolve into discussions about genetic makeup, experiential history, the momentum of proximate events ... the sorts of things defence lawyers are interested in.

SAVE THE WORLD

Such factors and elements are 4-dimensional by definition. This is why acts are not moral issues. Acts join other elements in conversations or conscious episodes intending to improve what will happen. What human beings might get up to is the sphere within which moral issues and normative conversations are relevant.

There is no need for convoluted arguments. The 3-dimensional phantasmagoria 'Tyson the rapist' did not survive the rape event. The issue is whether the Tyson-event (Mr. Tyson, past, present and future) is apt to generate similar 'sub-events' during its remaining course. "What is the likelihood of Mr Tyson re-offending?" becomes, in 4-dimensional terms: what is the likelihood of similar manifestations boiling up before the Tyson narrative subsides?

Societies and individuals have legitimate interest in such questions. Indeed, they have an obligation to think about these matters and do as much as possible to improve outcomes. This is where the mischief caused by 3-dimensional moralities is clearest. Many cultures execute or mutilate persons to accomplish justice and deterrence. There is no doubt that such spectacles provide individuals with reasons to stay on the straight and narrow. What is rarely considered is the ironic objection deterrence arguments position criminals to make: "I behaved badly because society failed to sufficiently punish people who were behaving badly. My conduct is due to the justice system's historical shortcomings. Therefore, you must not punish me."

Faced with such arguments, the judiciary has only one defence: "We must indeed do better. We will begin with you!"

In conclusion, judicial proceedings should

71

abandon 3-dimensional notions and regard accused beings in as large a sphere as possible. The justice system does some of this already. Extenuating experiences and circumstances are considered and some individuals are deemed blameless because of insanity or mental incompetence. We should take this to its logical conclusion. Only when the length and breadth of a 'Tyson Event' is on the docket, is it possible to understand the implications of antecedent circumstances such as childhood abuse. The notion of guilt should move from phantom individuals to their individuating circumstances. Individuals are symptoms of what is going on.

This analysis runs both ways. Paying attention to 4-dimensional circumstances does not mean guilty beings will start getting off Scott free or that societies will have no way to defend themselves. If we become more sensitive to the consequences of childhood abuse ..., this might exculpate accused individuals, but it also sets the stage for more fully assessing the harms flowing from such behaviour. This could enlarge the need to interdict 4-dimensional Tyson-events even as it excuses 3-dimensional manifestations.

The result would be a justice system with larger circumstances under possible indictment; a system better positioned to prevent harms and nurture moral outcomes.

We know that some cultures execute, mutilate and incarcerate dysfunctional or dangerous persons citing needs for public safety, vengeance and deterrence. These are inconsistent proceedings because they reflect ad hoc switching between 3-dimensional and 4-dimensional arguments. 3-dimensional beings are front and centre whenever the need to reward or punish dominates political and economic interests. Extenuating events are cited whenever indicted individuals can afford lawyers and when deterrence or public safety are on the table.

Public well-being is poorly served by this on-again, off-again, facile behaviour. Executions, institutional malfeasance, cruel and unusual punishment ... would be harder to rationalize without moral outrage enlarging pragmatic concerns past their natural force. Societies must deal with malignant issues, but summary interventions would occur less frequently in fully-fledged 4-dimensional contexts. Punishments would be meted out according to deterrence and public safety reasons; and deterrence might become less necessary as cultures become adept at 'stitch in time' interventions.

The 3-dimensional model would not have become universal had it not been doing useful work. Along with psychological benefits involving ego and feelings of self-hood, identifying persons as moral agents has undeniable socializing benefits. The 3-dimensional model places behaviour under the direction of putative moral and rational agents:—souls, immanent selves, precious motes in God's eye ... This is pleasant news, even if it cannot be true

Accordingly, an important question facing 4-dimensional advocates is whether notions of personal recognizance would survive the disappearance of 3-Dimensional 'immanent being' claims.

My intuition is that they would not only survive but become more robust! What is needed is a way of understanding that is broadly-based enough to diminish existential terrors, "God told me!" talk and "He said, she said" gossip.A way to begin builds upon French psychiatrist

HOW PHILOSOPHY COULD

Jacques Lacan's[9] characterization of apperception—the sense human beings have of being alive in a time and place. Lacan points out something interesting: our sense of being alive, of having a viewpoint, means that we can be aware of being aware but never see ourselves directly! We are *viewpoints* towards which sensations, perceptions and memories flow, *benchmarks* against which events are measured and projects organized.

If we instead understood ourselves in 4-dimensional terms, as decades-long named narratives, we would be reassured a thousand times over. We would become more aware of events bearing upon us, and more thoughtful of consequences flowing from what we get up to.

What's not to like?

Some conscious episodes generating 3-dimensional vantage points are happy, some not. The needle knitting these conscious episodes into narratives is the experience of being a point of view. If such experiences happen regularly—this almost always happens during childhood—robust notions of self-hood develop. If all goes well, the adults that emerge think well enough of themselves to carry on, but not so well that they insist upon floating down rivers like Cleopatra on her Nile barge.

When this equilibrium goes well, Grand People sometimes turn up. We know some of their names better than we know our own. Such people are rare, but a 4-dimensional stance offers such exciting possibilities that even people like you and I could enjoy rich lives.

Environmental benefits could also result from

---

9   https://en.wikipedia.org/wiki/Jacques_Lacan

moving to a 4-Dimensional model. Understandings would no longer be locked into an impossible present but could range back and forth across lifetimes, mining experiences and generating understandings previously overlooked. Such understandings would amount to a fresh vantage points and perhaps another trip down memory lane.

The commonsense world—crammed with objects, entities, and things to wish for—is a necessary stage on the road to its 4-Dimensional replacement. Here is how 3-Dimensional notions emerge. As human beings become aware of one another—think of passengers travelling the same direction and speed on multi-lane highways—tiny universes of simultaneity are generated. These passengers 'discover' that they are experiencing identical events. A boulder in my yard has been in my experience as long as i can remember. I point it out to you and see you seeing what I am pointing to. We talk about the boulder and notice that it seems to be external to both of us. We conclude that 'outside of us' not only exists but that it exists whether we are perceiving and talking about objects and entities.[10]

This is how the real world comes into existence. This world is a cultural achievement. It will exist as long as people keep talking about it, and not a second longer.

In the meantime, 'facts' fashioned during

---

10 Quantum events do not crystallize out of probabilities until observed. Since they only materialize for observers in the same room at the same time, they remain probabilities for potential observers in other rooms. This raises an interesting quid pro quo possibility: observations crystallize quantum events and observers of quantum events simultaneously.

HOW PHILOSOPHY COULD

these conversations can be used to identify who or what was responsible for this or that outcome. These facts also serve as stock-in-trade for corporations and nations. They underwrite currencies, wars and global undertakings. If the *Einstein's Tupperware Brain* project bears fruit, perhaps even genius will be understood sufficiently that it can be capitalized upon and become part of the global GNP.

Such investigations—and the correspondingly sophisticated arguments of moralizers, legislators and creationists—alert us to another danger. Deterministic explanations undermine 3-Dimensional notions of responsibility without correspondingly improving 4-dimensional understandings. If 3-dimensional understandings are dissolved with deterministic explanations reciting extenuating circumstances, the moral universe will shrink until it resembles the one experienced by primordial human beings. Even this could be optimistic. The modern rendering of amorality could be nothing like the primal version. Human beings have externalized, institutionalized and reverse-engineered responsibility-engendering activities into computer programs, business plans corporations and nations. These unprecedented circumstances, these quasi-life forms,will doubtlessly continue to 'progress and develop', using remnants of human beings as constituent parts.

In *Being and Nothingness*, Sartre speaks of 'a double, reciprocal incarnation'.

> I make myself flesh in order to
> impel the Other to realize for
> herself and for me her own flesh,
> and my caresses cause my flesh
> to be born for me in so far as it is

for the Other flesh causing her to
be born as flesh.

Such incarnations set the stage for an
alarming possibility. Anointing ourselves
agents with *a licence to choose* does not make
it true. As conscious agents we necessarily fail
to actualize intuitions and intentions that pop
into awareness. It is not that we are incapable
of timely responses. The problem is that we
have positioned ourselves as authors and
owners of responses and this conceit is
paralyzing us. We imagine ourselves initiating
and controlling responses. There is no easy
way to get this fantasy out of the way so
timely responses and projects can resume and
flourish.

Paralyzed, impotent, frantic ... we leave off
actually making responses and focus instead
upon passing intuitions and insights—and
bigotries and hatreds—among ourselves. Most
of the time, nothing comes of this. Intuitions
and insights recede from view in a day or a
week. Not always of course. Some insights are
seized upon by individuals eager to give as
many people as possible the business.

Most of the insights human beings have are
channelled into personal dead ends and cultral
backwaters. For thousands of years, this moral
and prudential vacuum has provided Big-
Thinkers with opportunities to convene
governments and corporations and organize
projects that would never have seen the light
of day otherwise.

The problem is becoming exponentially worse.
Billions of human beings are no longer capable
of putting themselves to work on their own
behalf. These populations amount to stables of
complaisant, unquestioning workers. They
insulate entrepreneurs and executives from
the messy business of putting insights into
practice. I think many historical projects would
have been amended or abandoned had their

authors been required to get their hands dirty! A day spent tending the ovens at Auschwitz might have clarified moral issues for Mr. Hitler and his cronies.

Now that almost all of us are looking for a job, morality and responsibility is nowhere to be seen. Construction workers on any project, soldiers in every war, guards supervising proceedings at Auschwitz, are invariably sanguine about what they are getting up to. They have plausible deniability. They operate under chains of command. The rest of the story is that the rest of human beings are drunk with the power the specialized and hapless confer upon them.

Lots of people have wonderful ideas. The problem is, intuitions about equity, spirituality, smaller ecological footprints ... are difficult to translate into profit-making, employment-generating projects. Such understandings sometimes survive among proselytizers and academics, but have little to do with the way the world works.

The problem has two components. The most important is that 3-Dimensional notions of agent-hood divide human beings into command and commanded functions. If I am an agent because I am conscious and capable of creating ideas, and then choosing whether to act upon them, I am divided within myself. I am a mind and a body, and my body is controlled by my mind. I choose to do something, then deputize my body to accomplish whatever I had in mind.

This partitioning also means I can deputize others to do my spade work and make my responses.

The consequences of this self-immolating mischief are everywhere we look. Intuitions need not result in responses by persons whose intuitions they are. They can be diverted into academic echo chambers or cultural activities wherein lectures, singing, marching ... replace actually doling stuff. Some responses are farmed out to corporations, governments, NGOs, platoons of people ... However, such responses occur only if there is profit to be made or publicly-funded money to be spent.

In other words, if insights do not lend themselves to commercial projects or enjoy political traction, they are likely to be stillborn. The result is a growing imbalance between profitable, power-brokering ideas that spawn corporations and nations and wonderful rational and moral ideas that are either stillborn or on life support.

Another consequence of this partitioning involves the loathing thinkers and doers tend to develop for one another. Each sees the other as dysfunctional. Thinkers regard doers as primitive and unimaginative. Doers regard thinkers as effete twits. Both are right! Each requires what they dismiss in the other to be whole!

The manner in which expectations inform and transform societies has been thought about many times. David Riesman's 1950 book *The Loney Crowd* can be read as depicting various consequences of 3-dimensional thinking in different socioeconomic circumstances According to Riesman, the initial wave of immigrants to North America were 'old country' outer-directeds, rich in traditions and steeped in class-based expectations.

These expectations were given short shrift in the New World. The vast, untamed country demanded inner-directedness. Presto! Within one generation, frontiersman, cowboys, self-reliant, self-directing sons and daughters ... started turning up. These were reluctantly heroic individuals however. They were having too many conscious episodes to suit them but had *no choice* except soldiering on. The results included two centuries of vitality, creativity and economic exuberance.

During the last fifty years of the 20th century, North Americans were finally able to abandon inner-directedness in favour of Riesman's remaining possibility. We became *other-directeds*, our priorities and values dictated by commercial messages and by what Noam Chomsky termed *The Manufacture of Consent*.

During the inner-directed phase of these proceedings 1st World populations invented amazing technologies and generated enormous wealth. These assets encouraged gifted individuals (like the poor, always with us) to contrive ways to transfer most of this wealth into their hands.

This went more smoothly than they probably hoped because they had an unexpected ally. The rest of us, uneasy about the number of conscious episodes entailed by subsistence activities and personal responsibility, were eager to give up inner-directed lifestyles. In addition, the other-directed lives salesmen and politicians were recommending looked like more fun than the onerous, relentless work our parents and grandparents had reminisced about. The lives promised by industrial revolutionists resembled *Heaven on Earth*, wombs with Utopian views.

Even so, why would robustly-independent, prosperous populations embrace infantile, dependent lives? Why not invest new technologies in further independence? I think part of the answer is that, deep down, we know that we have never willed a thought into existence or consciously shepherded a project to completion. All we know is that thoughts keep bubbling up, work keeps getting done and we are occasionaly aware of what is happening. Embracing other-directed forms of life: chains of command, *force majeure* economies ... allowed us to stop making dubious agent claims before someone blows the whistle!

In summary, moral intuitions are hard to take public and monetize and unlikely to be put into practice by individuals accustomed to deflecting responsibility. At the same time, money-making and power-brokering possibilities are vigorously investigated. Human beings survived this lopsidedness for centuries because moral and prudential lessons were unconsciously transmitted across generations as cultural practices. This came to an end with the Industrial Revolution, urbanization and globalization. Young people today are completely exposed to the machinations and exploits of a tiny proportion of human beings—some speak of one per cent.

What strategies would the 4-dimensional model recommend in the face of these troubles? As a thought experiment, I suggest reviewing the merits of western-style incarceration vs. more notorious practices ... flogging, stoning, the cutting off of hands, when individuals have been found guilty of criminal offences. Western feminists have been known to recommend castration for rapists, but most shy away from such remedies. Mothers prefer MADD projects, perhaps recognizing that the fellow being castrated could be her own dear lad, now that he has wheels.

From a 4-dimensional standpoint, there is no logical difference between removing a portion of a person's 'spatial extent' (by castration or some other amputation) vs. excising a year or twenty years of temporal extent. Significantly, amputation and imprisonment coincide when individuals are executed and their temporal and spatial extents collapse simultaneously.

Cultures in developed nations frown upon flogging, castration, removing hands ... claiming that such practices are bestial. This sentiment depends upon the claim that a person who has 'done her time' is the same person who had been locked up—hopefully, rehabilitated, improved, educated, socialized. This raises interesting questions:

- Are rehabilitated individuals the same persons they would be if they had not been rehabilitated? If so, what does rehabilitation consist of? If not, what do persons consist of? Are we dipping a toe in 4-dimensional waters with such questions?

- Institutionalization is widely understood as undermining the therapeutic value of incarceration. Communities springing up whenever malcontents, deviants and crooks ... spend time together encourage recidivism.

- It costs money to jail people. These costs are transferred to taxpayers in regressive ways. As well, poor people and minority populations are more likely to find themselves incarcerated.

- The benefits of deterrence and rehabilitation are progressively distributed. The wealthy have more to gain from an orderly society.

So the question is: are populations better served by 'castration' or incarceration protocols? Would Mr.Tyson have been advantaged? It might have been deemed sufficient to remove only one of his testicles, perhaps placing the second on probation.

Tyson could then have gotten on with his life without suffering institutionalization, criminalization, loss of career opportunities ... all unquantifiable concomitants of incarceration. Measured (½) castration might have mitigated testosterone-management issues and would have avoided the public costs of his incarceration.

Incarceration advocates need to ask whether 'temporal surgeries'—a year or ten sliced out of an individual's life—is not more draconian, less efficacious and more problematic morally than spatial excisions.

If societies find that they must punish individuals, there is another reason spatial amputations might be the way to go. We have no way of knowing what proportion of a person's life a 'temporal excision' represents. A person serving 5 years may die a month after release, and will have effectively served a life sentence. Even without this difficulty, a life sentence for a young person is different from a life sentence for a middle-aged or old person.

None of these difficulties arise when 'spatial extents' are laid hold of.

I am offering this somewhat tongue-in-cheek story as a way of suggesting why 4-dimensional responses to criminal events are the way to go.

– 5 –

A 4-dimensional understanding of organisms, thunderstorms, climate warming processes, the antics of corporations ... could improve moral, rational and practical outcomes. We would no longer speak of discrete entities passing through time. Be existing, entities have used their allotment. Persons would be seen as narratives. Birth and death mark the beginning and ending of these narratives—the way waves rise out of bodies of water, endure for a time and collapse back.

Subjective experiences are the fruit of these narratives melding with hurricanes, nations, corporations, sunshine and other persons. They stitch themselves together out of conscious episodes. They provide glimpses into what is going on from within what is going on.

In this story, the world that seems real and external is generated and imagined into existence by beings like you and I gossiping about private experiences. To return a final time to the highway metaphor, drivers spend time signalling, encouraging and adjuring ... one another. Articles and messages are lobbed from vehicle to vehicle, necessitating estimations of 'distance' so that persons and footballs intersect.

Persons intersect as well. The results are often lovely. Occasionally however, intersections are so disruptive that events are terminated. This does not mean obliterated. Whatever narratives consisted of, their consequences will participate eternally in what is going on.

4-dimensional thinking offers another 'quantum of solace'. You and I do not exist the way we have been thinking. We are not tourists travelling about the world. We are not separated beings leading separate lives.

Finally, 4-dimensional morality develops two intuitions. The first is that events have consequences. The second is that moral spheres only exist during conscious episodes wherein consequences are being anticipated, contemplated and settled upon. Once this process concludes and acts occur, moral spheres collapse into what is going on.

Now that milk has been spilt and consequences are spreading everywhere moral talk no longer makes sense. Whether acts are large or small, trivial or momentous, consequences soon become unfathomable. Sometimes this is because they are imperceptible. Sometimes they are so large and convoluted as to be incomprehensible. The Second World War, the nuclear bombs dropped on Hiroshima and Nagasaki ..., are such acts.

In the face of these difficulties, the only morally defensible path is to maximize wholesome outcomes as best we can. This ambition should not be restricted to but must include human beings.

How could this be achieved? The "do unto others" Golden Rule provides a clue. During conscious episodes—before acts are committed and moral possibilities remain— human beings should strive for divergent (4-dimensional) rather than convergent (3-dimensional) understandings.

Einstein changed the way we understand the universe. The next step is to consider the Theory of Relativity's implications for how we understand ourselves.

End Game

*Reading through my diary of
things to worry about, I came
across the following twenty-year
old note-to-self.*

On February 25, 1996, a middle-aged, middle-
class woman I know drove her thirteen year
old son and his friend one hundred miles along
Highway # 7 in Ontario to play in a hockey
game.

Along the way, she might have observed
somber-faced individuals in garages and
basement—OPSEU members preparing picket
signs for duty the following day. She probably

did not however. She was, after all, filled with the satisfaction that comes from spending time with robust young boys and providing wholesome experiences to boot! Who does not think sportsmanship, teamwork and athletic excellence are worthwhile?

Yet there remains the business of posters being prepared for a strike and, behind that, the widespread public conviction that Ontario Premier Mike Harris' common sense revolution made sense.

What do strike preparations have to do with an innocent trip along an Ontario highway? The thing that occurs to me is that, while we go about our serenely busy lives, the middle-class we belong to, or aspire to belong to, is being decimated.

To put figures to it, North Americans have been enjoying a 20-40-40 economy for decades. These numbers describe the proportion of people in the upper, middle and lower classes. They should be read in the context of another statistic. In western nations, household wealth distribution has been 40-40-20 across upper, middle and lower class populations. Combining these numbers tells an important story. 20% of North Americans enjoy 40% of the wealth, the bottom 40% must make do with 20%, leaving 40% for the 40% in the middle.

This is how it has been in western nations during most of the 20th century. However, these numbers began skewing further in favor of the upper-class in the 1970s. It was not only that the upper-class was becoming wealthier, middle-class purchasing power was shrinking, and even fully-employed lower-class individuals faced increasing housing and food security issues.

Even so, North Americans and Europeans seemed content. Even if economic warts were turning up, the lower class remained appreciably better off than billions elsewhere. Many recognized that they were escaping the hard work and rural life styles their parents and grandparents had reminisced about.

In broad strokes, historical economies are easy to describe. Until a few hundred years ago, there was no middle-class to speak of: 5% of the population had 95% of the wealth and 95% had 5%. This sounds no better and perhaps worse than life today for poor people around the world. There was a difference however. For most of human history, there was not much wealth in circulation. Most of the world remained unexplored, unaccounted for and belonged to no one. A world that mostly belongs to no one is a world somewhat available to everyone. Was this a poorer world? The answer is yes and no. Progress and development is all about transforming public resources into privately held assets. As the world become wealthier in terms of monetized assets It becomes poorer in terms of public resources, sometimes referred to as *the commons*.

Assets are inventoried in currency terms. Cars, houses, farms ... are worth this much money. One way money differs from resources is that money reflects the distillation of resources into liquid forms that can be stored, accumulated and spent. Money enables people to enjoy adventures and undertake otherwise impossible projects. Traveling to the moon, the Large Hadron Collider and nuclear weapons would not be on the mankind's score sheet without money.

As you have doubtlessly noticed, money also allows individuals and corporations to invest in further wealth-generating projects. This does not sound too bad (especially if jobs are promised) until we remember that wealthy individuals and corporations can command the activities of people who do not have money but must acquire some to survive. In today's world, people with lots of money control the activities and, more importantly, the prospects of people without money. This is a new form of enslavement. This state of affairs has advantages over historical slavery. Modern slaves rarely understand their predicament which means they are spared psychological distress. They are also more docile than historical slave populations. There is another important benefit for modern slavers. They get to go about giving people the business proudly. The more successful they become, the greater the proportion of human beings at their beck and call, the more they are celebrated.

More generally, mankind's balance sheet boasts many achievements. What is missing is any systematic accounting of liabilities that have been incurred to achieve these results. Environmental degradation, extinctions, global warming, resource depletion … are dismissed as externalized costs. The enslavement of billions to the ambitions of corporations and individuals owning them surely counts as a liability. The fact that, in 2017, Donald Trump and Kim Jong-un could strut mankind into nuclear Armageddon should be taken into account when totting up progress and development's score card.

Things were not that good a century ago either. The First World War was raging. Human beings were killing one another in increasingly fiendish ways, including mustard gas. There were no nuclear weapons however—two decades would elapse before Hiroshima and Nagasaki ushered in the atomic age and the possibility of nuclear Armageddon.

One hundred years ago, there was one wholesome political and economic factor in play that no longer exists. Until the last half of the 20th century, most human beings depended upon subsistence activities, wage employments, family and community economies and commons resources for their livelihood. We hunted for and grew food. We contrived shelters and security measures. We socialized, reproduced, played music, drank beer, defecated ... without doffing a hat or paying a dime.

This left much to be desired. As Thomas Hobbes observed, human life has often been nasty, brutish and short. However, earlier generations had a resource that was so important and seminal that it never crossed anyone's mind. During the centuries when nations had minuscule GNP numbers, no one had any idea how much value human beings were producing. Nations had no idea how robust their economies were because people were doing things among themselves in spontaneously-occurring underground ways.

This is an important clue! This meant that profits, tax revenues and dependent people were less available to governments, corporations and megalomaniac individuals.

The fact that similarly small GNP numbers are rapidly becoming facts of life for a growing proportion of people should be regarded with alarm. If subsistence activities are ignored, the poor in times past were worse off than their counterparts today. A second look suggests that they were better off in important ways. The middle-class did not exist in sufficient numbers that the poor could imagine joining their ranks. The wealthy have always led splendid lives, but their joys and antics were not broadcasted into billions of living rooms every day to remind the rest of us that our lives leave much to be desired.

What is also seductive is that even poor people today have entertainments and medical resources unavailable to kings and queens a few hundred years ago. These achievements camouflage the changing nature of poverty. I propose that poor people today have a bleaker prospect than their counterparts a century ago. The communities, families and subsistence options everyone once took for granted have vanished.

The most pressing reason this should concern us is that a rich/poor world is the direction we are headed. Automation and global trade agreements are placing middle and lower class populations in ever-sharper competition for ever fewer jobs. Emerging nation workers can rarely afford to purchase products they help bring into existence. It was ever thus, but gardens, goats, communities and cultural activities once made dignified existence possible even so

In addition to immolating domestic populations, the managers of 1st World economies are increasingly sophisticated about siphoning wealth from 3rd world nations. These incursions include advertising, manufacturing and commercial practices developed since the 19th century. Pre-industrial revolution populations across Europe and North America were transformed into hapless and therefore reliable wealth-generators by processes involving urbanization, specialization and the loss of subsistence activities. These stratagems and off-the-shelf technologies are making emerging nation populations easy prey.

The fruits of these exploits are not being distributed equitably across 1st world populations. To be sure, western consumers have been enjoying cheap goods and the benefit of having pollution-spewing manufacturing activities occur over there.

These are day by day benefits. Year over year

HOW PHILOSOPHY COULD

consequence are not so friendly. Exploiting emerging nations has also been undermining 1ˢᵗ world employments and destabilizing global politics. Nations crippled with unbalanced supply/demand capabilities and disgruntled middle class populations are sitting on a powder keg. The existence of the global economy rationalizes still more outsourcing and automating to keep Ponzi economies inflated. The more of this that happens the worse economic problems become.

As the purchasing power of most people declines in western nations and fails to materialize elsewhere, pencils must be sharpened if corporations are to survive. Globalization completes the circle. The next order of business is to shrink life-styles until the world GNP becomes sustainable. This is being accomplished with tried and true, intuitively-acceptable mechanism. The more efficient nations become at producing goods and services without reasonably-paid human involvement, the poorer people become on average!

This spiraling-down dilemma is exacerbated—or lubricated—by three factors: the growing concentration of wealth in a few hands; the growing cost of servicing public debt; and the growing difficulty of maintaining services and infrastructure when the usual person's real-dollar income is declining.

Unless something intervenes, middle-class populations—and the possibility of a neither rich nor poor future—may be a blip on mankind's dreary 95% poor/5% wealthy landscape.

What do hockey mothers, athletic sons and OPSEU picket signs have to do with this? The answer is that only middle-class individuals can save the middle-class. The wealthy have priorities that serve them very well. They almost certainly understand that middle class life-styles must be collapsed if wealth is going to continue to mean anything. The poor must struggle every day to survive and, if resources permit, distract themselves with entertainments and addictions.

The only possibility involves middle-class individuals recognizing that they cannot all become wealthy, winners, or leaders.[11]Modern capitalist economies are zero-sum Ponzi schemes. When individuals become wealthy, a large number must become poorer. When a few million become stupendously wealthy, billions must be correspondingly impoverished.

The good news, the insight lower and middle class populations should seize upon, is that these troubles are not caused by greedy people becoming wealthy or powerful by following gut instincts. The greedy exist because the rest of us have been handing over the value of our work and then expecting the wealthy we are creating to look after us. The wealthy are victims as well. You and I have been making them ugly and dangerous. There is an expression for this: "Power corrupts. Absolute power corrupts absolutely."

This has been going on for so long that wealth-creating practices have been baked into economic and political practices to the point that no one has to even think about them. Progressive practices (e.g., percentage-driven financial instruments and union contracts) transfer the benefits of economics activities up the entitlement ladder. Regressive practices direct consequences and harms to the rest of us.

---

11   http://www.bbc.com/future/story/20170418-how-western-civilisation-could-collapse

HOW PHILOSOPHY COULD

For a time, the middle class looked like an exception and light at the end of the tunnel. Alas, the middle class has been functioning as a loss-leader, seducing populations into urban centres where they could be fleeced and have the wool pulled over their eyes.

The global economy is taking the economic immolation the middle class made possible to its logical conclusion and applying it to the middle class itself.

It does not have to be this way. The middle class provided a glimpse of a neither rich nor poor world. What happened to this lovely possibility? Part of the problem is that individuals are rarely content, no matter how well appointed their lives. Some of this involves habituation—the attention-freeing mechanism that means placid frogs can be boiled alive if bath-water temperature rises slowly enough. Significantly, the wealthy have never been content either. This tells us everything we need to know about life-styles and happiness.

The fact that rich keep raising the bar defining what counts as enough permeates everything human beings get up to. Now that technology gives us the means to listen and watch day and night, we have all become voyeurs. No matter how sordid or banal, we can't take our eyes off of what the wealthy get up to and what they wear (or omit to wear) while doing so. Without saying a word, they convince us that our circumstances need improvement—no matter how luxurious our lives compared to our parents, or to the millions lacking a pot to piss in or a window to throw the results through

Even so, even now, we could still take up the middle-class, middle-ground possibility and begin extricating ourselves from corporate agendas and the life-style fantasies. We could explore other possibilities. We could invest in local well-being. We could start growing food locally, changing one another's oil, cutting one another's hair ....

There is no reason local economies could not produce a good deal of what is needed. The more of this we manage the more immune families and communities—and nations of families and communities—become to central economy reversals, corporate re-locations, legislated claw-backs and commercial malfeasance.

I am not suggesting that most needs could—or should—be locally-sourced. A start could be made however, and every step would be an improvement. A surprising proportion might be deemed manageable however, especially when people notice how well-off they are becoming when more of the value of their work is retained within families and communities.

What makes this possibility compelling is the stark nature of the alternative. An increasing proportion of human beings are urbanized and can no longer engage in subsistence activities. Indeed, they hardly do anything for themselves. How does this make sense? In cities it is impossible to survive without money, and money is increasingly difficult to come by.

Again, what does this have to do with mothers, sons and 100 mile trips to play hockey? Part of the answer involves the OPSEU pickets being prepared as a public sector union prepares to do battle. In 1996, there were more than 60,000 provincial employees in Ontario, and the province was on record as wishing to be rid of between 13,000 and 25,000 of them. To this end, the Harris government had designated a number of jobs as essential and passed scab-enabling legislation.

The Harris government was voted into office with a strong mandate. The values, expectations and anxieties involved would eventually grow large enough to trigger BREXIT and lead to the Donald Trump presidency in 2017. Even twenty years ago, walking a picket lines required courage and resolve.

- Strikers knew they might never return to their jobs.

- Strikers risk authenticating the government's hard-line stance. They demonstrate—at least in the short term—that services can be delivered with fewer, often unsophisticated employees.

- Strikers partially finance eventual settlements out of lost wages.

How did this state of affairs come into existence? Human beings like to point to external factors to explain problems. We are reluctant to ask whether we are ourselves complicit in what is going on.

I think this is a mistake. First, we cannot all be innocent bystanders or victims. The second reason this is a mistake is that we dis-empower ourselves. If we identify even a thread of personal complicity in a problem, we suddenly find ourselves positioned to do something about it. We could eliminate, or at least diminish, our own contribution! This might not solve much, but doing something is better than doing nothing—and one often sees step two from the vantage point of having completed step one.

The OPSEU strike preparations and road trip along Highway #7 suggests another possibility. The values and priorities driving economies and political events are transmitted among communities and across generations. The mother, son and friend looking forward to an evening playing Canada's national sport is just such a cultural vector. A surprising number of lessons are being communicated. For example, there is the idea that one must go somewhere, enter into some formal organization or institution, get permission from someone ... to play a game or have a meaningful experience.

What is being instilled is the dictum: do not even think about doing spontaneous, natural, wholesome ... stuff on your own recognizance! Events do not count unless they are formally organized, supervised, refereed and unless win-lose scores are recorded.

Parents driving young athletes to practices and games are acting out another unfortunate notion. They are not modeling life-long athleticism. They are demonstrating that the window of vigorous life is a decade, perhaps two, long.

These lessons are underscored by the short-lived careers of professional athletes. The moral is clear: there is no point in getting involved in athletic endeavors unless one has supernatural genes. We might as well retire to our couches. We might as well harness our big brains and superb reflexes to figuring out remote-control devices.

The consequences include a rising tide of obesity, heart disease, diabetes ... These are sports-related injuries that come on slowly enough that we get used to them day by day. Later on, when muscles have atrophied, bones de-calcified, balance, reflexes, mental acuity ... withered, we may have an identifiable sports-related injury. We slip and fall, get trundled off to a hospital, or perhaps a palliative care ward.

HOW PHILOSOPHY COULD

En route, it might occur to us that we have been in palliative care since our parents stopped driving us somewhere to compete and invited us to sit with them and watch a game.

Such mischief requires professional organizing. The sports establishment serves up a constant stream of entertainment: competitions, commentaries, injuries, occasional deaths and, now and then, drug busts. These events combine with athletes' fabulous salaries, exotic lives ... to make vicarious, voyeuristic lives seem legitimate and worthwhile. All we ask is that sports-governing bodies keep drugs out of the picture! We want our pornographic thrills pure and clean, thank you very much!

There are political benefits as well. As world-records move beyond ordinary reach, superhuman athletes help the rest of us understand why our lives are not going well. We are not poor because we are being messed with, farmed or exploited. We are poor because we are incompetent.

If more evidence is needed it can be found on couches, in sports bars, in stadiums, at shopping malls ... rotund fans armed with vigorous opinions and trenchant analyses, raptly watching athletes raise achievement bars into the stratosphere.

Every community appears to have been co-opted into these proceedings. I live near Stirling Ontario, a small town if ever there was one. On the road approaching Stirling from the east, a sign exclaims that travelers are entering "The Proud Home of ... (4) NHL Stars!"

Here's a political score card for End Gamers:

- Life sorts people into winners and losers.

- There are more losers than winners.

- Lessons abound: "Suck it up!" "No whining!" "No pain, no gain!" "It's not about how many times you get knocked down, it's about how many times you get back up!"

In such circumstances, joining a team is recommended. There will still be more losers than winners, but there is strength and camaraderie in numbers. When defeats occur, the team, the organization—even the fans— understand themselves as part of the equation. Responsibility for losing gets shared around.

Amazingly, in a modern version of the loaves and fishes miracle, every winning participant in a competition, including every fan, gets to claim a full measure of credit when victory occurs.

Accordingly:

- individuals should join as many teams as possible, or become a fan and strive to be the best fan possible;

- individuals should expect to lose most of the time;

- equality issues are satisfied if everybody has an equal chance to be a winner.

In these high stakes games, an occasional athlete must be thrown off of the bus for the greater good. Thus, Lance Armstrong and Ben Johnson were sacrificed to resurrect their sports' virginal status—even though drug use was rampant when they were competing, and continues today.

Finally, sports activities are said to be good for

decorum and public order. Athletes work out aggressions that might otherwise find dangerous outlets. With the help of mirror neurons, fans enjoy similar cathartic benefits.

An even more important benefit may be occurring. Even if they are not sports fans, people cannot help internalizing 'life lessons' about fairness, the logical nature of win/lose ratios and the importance of being a good sport. In a global economy sorting human beings into a few winners and lots of losers, the value of "sucking it up" has never been so important.

These benefits, and the sports establishment's connection with OPSEU picketers, governments and corporations, depend upon thinking in terms of competing teams, opposing interests, rules-of-engagement and winning tactics. Elections and union-management negotiations are parsed to determine which side played the best game.

If this rendering of justice and probity continues, the possibility that ordinary well-being could improve if political and economic proceedings were collegial rather than confrontational will never be thought of.

Sports-themed understandings are also in play internationally. Nations are teams of citizens. Corporations compete for customers, and governments function as referees making sure rules are followed. The only time cooperation and collegiality are valued is when nations go abroad seeking foreign contracts or trade agreements. Representatives talk about their nations as the best place for corporations to give domestic populations the business—in return for reciprocal access!

After all, fair is fair.

Two-Engine Economies

Let me conclude by sketching a way forward. For at least a century, there has been debate over whether capitalism or socialism is the best way to organize human affairs. If we overlook that socialism or communism has never been tested (thinly-veiled totalitarianism a la the USSR, China, Cuba ... notwithstanding), there is a way to think about economies that has not been tested.

There is no reason nations could not organize two-engine, bi-polar economies and enjoy the benefits of capitalism and socialism simultaneously. Since western nations are already *Big Capitalism,* a bi-polar economy would only require adding *small capitalism* initiatives.

By definition, these would be community, local, regional ... undertakings. Western nations—especially middle-class populations in western nations—need to recognize that progress and development has been creating 3rd world populations in their midst. These populations consist of the unemployed and poorly employed in cities and in marginalized rural areas.

Not only is there no solution on the horizon for these people, their prospect will only worsen. In two-engine economies these individuals could transition into local initiatives and—in a kind of economic diaspora—transfer energy, productive capacity and needs from moribund cities to villages and rural communities.

Bi-polar economies offer an alternative to traditional welfare (and even guaranteed income) responses to failures of equity and opportunity. Communist or socialist economies have equally notorious problems including corruption, lack of initiative and responsibility on the part of workers and supervisors. In both circumstances, two-engine economies would retain the vigor capitalism brings to the table while gaining the stability and safety-net benefits of subsistence and local economy activities.

Each engine in these economies would function independently. Each would be an antidote and countervail to weaknesses in the other. Bi-polar economies would retain capitalism's ingenuity and capacity to finance large undertakings. Nations would gain a second value-generating and tax-revenue stream: local or secondary economies with or without distinctive currencies.

There is a good chance that underground economy participants would be persuaded to invest their talents, assets and needs in local possibilities!

Intuitively, two-engine economies would be more stable. They would retrieve the resilience western economies enjoyed until recently, when robust levels of subsistence activities were occurring.

The fact that this level of historical resourcefulness did not ward off the Great Depression demonstrates the need for enlarged local economies to help nations ride out, or prevent, economic storms.

Bi-polar economies would provide wholesome ways to respond to unemployment problems. Environmental footprints would be smaller because more stuff would be produced and consumed locally. Individuals would instinctively embrace green technologies, durable products and low-overhead distribution practices.

Presently, when employments are lost because of progress and development, automation or outsourcing, displaced people must be supported by forms of socialism—welfare, unemployment insurance, charities and food-banks. In bi-polar nations, these individuals could transition to local economies. The public costs of demoralizing, stigmatizing safety-net expenditures could be invested in local-economy assets and infrastructure.

These initiatives could dovetail with technical and trade-school programs and facilitate the reintegration of people leaving prisons or marching home from war.

Finally, the emergence of two-engine economies in 1st world nations would provide examples and technologies relevant to emerging nations.

The middle-class has been collapsing for at least a half-century in 1st world nations. This is an enormous problem and also a wonderful opportunity. This collapse signals that something is profoundly wrong with the way we are giving one another the business. We cannot just stop the economic train without disastrous consequences. However, nothing prevents nations from formally implementing complementary local economies.

This rendition of capitalism would incorporate two well-established systems. The solution to Big Capitalism vs. Big Socialism could be as simple as retaining Big Capitalism and adding complementary Little Capitalisms.

Two-engine economies also make sense in the context of international trade agreements and globalization. Arguments for globalization are almost always guilty of *fallacies of composition.* They assume that trade agreements can be put in place without harming domestic employments and purchasing power. There is already plenty of evidence that this is not true, but economies of scale and political pressures in commodity-producing nations mean globalization will continue come Hell or High Water.

If the majority of human beings are to prosper under *urbanization* and *globalization,* we have to figure out ways to distribute wealth equitably. Nothing about capitalism automatically distributes the benefits of progress and globalization across populations. Capitalism's benefits tend to be *progressive,* its consequences *regressive.* The rich get richer, the poor, poorer.

An antidote to the harms of globalization could involve government-convened efforts to achieve *localization.*

The alternative is a future wherein nations vanish as sovereign entities and as places where more than a few lead interesting lives.

Democracy as End Game Referee

There used to be jokes that began "Meanwhile, back at the ranch ..." and concluded with something like "the Lone Ranger, disguised as a sheet of paper, slipped under the door."

In today's world, there are few ranches and subsistence activities are vanishing in lock-step with middle-ground possibilities. Significantly, interest in extending democracy and capitalism into communistic, socialistic and authoritarian nations has been growing in tandem with these developments. This became unmistakable when the USSR broke into constituent parts late in 1991. The world watched in amazement as the Soviet Union disintegrated into fifteen separate countries. This was hailed as a victory for freedom, a triumph of democracy over totalitarianism, and evidence of the superiority of capitalism over socialism.

Each of the resulting countries (roughly, the countries amalgamated into the USSR in the first place) appear determined to enjoy the fruits of capitalism and democracy. There was a problem however. These populations had nursed ethnic and sectarian grievances through almost a century of forced conviviality and these hatreds started flaring up. Even so, industrialization and western style capitalism rooted up and a new wealthy class emerged.

The break up of the USSR and subsequent spurt of capitalism beg the same question: why is democracy suddenly springing up everywhere? Is it possible that the world is enjoying a renaissance of spirituality or morality? Nothing else going on supports any such hope. Well-appointed barns and comfortable quarters do not mean farmers have changed their position regarding cattle, pigs or chickens.

I think the key to understanding these developments involves replacing *revolution* with *disintegration* in descriptions of what has been going on. Historically, revolutions have been bottom-up events. They embody whatever ideological alternatives revolutionaries imagine will correct inequities or injustices.

The people authoring USSR-style breakups do not seem to have such ambitions.

Who are these people? Most seem angry, anxious, worried, disgusted ... citizens very like rank and file revolutionaries everywhere. However, today's leaders do not seem to have noble agendas on their minds. Historically, the people at the centre of revolutions hoped for better things for their fellow citizens and nations. Disintegrators see the status quo not as something to repair but as an opportunity to exploit. They see fellow citizens as assets or obstacles. They see themselves better off when new pecking orders crystallize.

In the case of the disintegration of the USSR, fifteen new pecking orders beckoned, each vitalized with infusions of capitalism and democracy. Such revolutionaries can be thought of as *terrorists with secular plans*. A terrorist is any person with a non-negotiable agenda who is prepared to use sanctions or the threat of sanctions to get his or her way

The interest groups, the power brokers, the wealthy ... who catalyzed the breakup of the USSR were nothing like the revolutionaries that brought the USSR into existence.

How do modern revolutionaries hope to achieve their ambitions? The results are unanimous! No form of governance succeeds as well as democratic capitalism at harnessing populations to the producing and consuming of goods and generating profits. In the decades leading up to 1991, the leaders of the USSR could not have failed to realize that they could not compete, economically or militarily, with capitalist nations.

Another turning-point occurred when capitalist nations gave master-class demonstrations that democracy was no threat to wealthy minorities or the rule of the many by the few. This lesson was underscored when the Second World War ended ignominiously for a totalitarian government, goose-stepping soldiers notwithstanding. The same war provided reassurance that democratic nations could get millions on the march should the need arise.

In short, the motivation for globalizing democracy and capitalism includes old-fashioned greed and envy. The leaders of non-democratic nations have been comparing their lot with that of their capitalist, democratic counterparts and coming up short!

There has to be some such explanation. With apologies to Steven Pinker,[12] talk of *better angels* and evolving morality does not explain what is occurring. A more plausible explanation is that urbanization, specialization and economic dependency means citizens can finally be trusted to vote for the status quo, and that it makes good sense to let them do so.

Occupational specialization, the corollary of urbanization and industrialization, has also been contributing to democracy's acceptability. What decisions do specialized populations feel competent to discuss or make? Specialists are amoral. Being

---

12   Pinker, S. (2011). The Better Angels of our Nature. New York, NY: Viking.

HOW PHILOSOPHY COULD

responsible is like being pregnant: one cannot be a little of either. A nation of specialists is a nation of morally-sterile individuals organized into corporations, institutions, producers and consumers. The things organizations get up to are, by definition, not the responsibility of constituent parts. This can be easily demonstrated. Whenever poked at with some environmental or social justice stick, specialists sing out their "just doing my job" refrain.

This means that any agenda whatsoever can be pursued with no one to demur. When the USSR disintegrated, hundreds if not thousands of nuclear engineers and scientists found themselves at loose ends. North Korea's Kim dynasty apparently made offers many of them could not refuse.

> ... after the collapse of the Soviet Union, ... out-of-work Russian rocket scientists began seeking employment in North Korea. Soon, a new generation of North Korean missiles began to appear, all knockoffs of Soviet designs. Though flight tests were sparse, American experts marveled at how the North seemed to avoid the kinds of failures that typically strike new rocket programs, including those of the United States in the late 1950s.[13]

In 2017, in the guise of US President Donald Trump and North Korea's Kim Jung-un, nuclear-armed turkeys are strutting and gobbling as if tomorrow does not matter.

13 http://www.backlander.ca/trump-inherits-a-secret-cyberwar-against-north-korean-missiles-the-new-york-times/

SAVE THE WORLD

Not only are specialists amoral, not having broadly-based moral or rational understandings does not mean that they are humble. Specialists often seem to compensate for narrow spheres of competence with belligerence, a sense of entitlement and conspicuous consumption. They vote for individuals representing their (lack of) moral values and promising to shore up notions of exceptionalism and entitlement.

Specialists gain a sense of identity and security by cleaving to occupational and national boundaries. These demarcations allow them to identify one another and organize into factions and sects.

There is another problem. Since specialists focus upon portions of what is known, they are best defined by what they do not know and by what they are not responsible for. The reason is that there is no point in describing a specialist in terms of what he or she does or is responsible for. Only identically-trained individuals could understand what is being said. However, it is always possible, and sometimes useful, to say what specialists should not be getting up to.

In other words, specialists can only be monitored to make sure they do not venture beyond spheres of competence. This is manageable because, while specialists have no idea what other specialists are getting up to, they have no trouble identifying trespassers in their domains! (This is formalized in unionized workplaces with detailed post descriptions.)

In spite of these limitations and consequences, specialists have no trouble making a grand case for themselves. Lacking any understanding of what is going on, denying all responsibility for what is going on, specialists still claim to be an expert part of whatever nation they belong to. This is the definition of patriotism! This is why Americans regard themselves and their nation as exceptional, as a shining light in a darkening world, even though many cannot locate the USA on a map of this world.

Canadians have no such confusion. While equally specialized and irresponsible, every Canadian knows that Canada is north of the USA!

The result is that nations, corporations, religions ... can be populated with individuals with little understanding of the juggernauts they are constituting. All individuals need to know to be fully-fledged, eager participants is that they are part of an organization, nation or, to use a term in the news these days, caliphate.

What does this have to do with globalizing democracy? I think it is fair to say that big-Democracy, big Capitalism proponents have little interest in the spiritual or economic well-being of even their fellow citizens, much less the citizens of other nations. They are, however, fascinated with capitalism's ability to build factories and shopping centers and fill them with profitable workers and consumers.

They are equally interested In the way democracies transfer responsibility for excesses and inequities from beneficiaries to victims. Now that a critical proportion of human beings are urbanized, specialized and dependent, human beings can be trusted with a vote in what is happening. Democracies can be likened to the sacraments of confession and absolution. During campaigns, politicians confess one another's sins. On Absolution Day, voters assume responsibility for everything that occurred since the last election. New governments are installed. Fresh rounds of sinning begin.

SAVE THE WORLD

Democracy is the best possible form of governance: one person, one vote, and every person enfranchised. Global democratization could also be the worst thing that has ever happened. The world's wealthy have been assessing governance models. They are not doing this because they are worried about your and my future. They have been admiring democratic capitalism's capacity to spawn millionaires and keep them safe.

Such motives cannot be talked about in public forums, much less during election campaigns. Democracy became the flavor of the day because it admirably deflects responsibility for what is going on upon the victims of what is going on.

In totalitarian circumstances, unmistakable responsibility attaches to individuals holding purse strings and reins of power. These individuals know that they are lightning rods. They do not have institutionalized processes dissolving or deflecting public hostility.

Democracies provide such mechanisms. In democracies, springy new hope is never more than an election away. Because of this, fall guys rarely notice how long their winter of discontent has lasted.

Incidental Publications

In retrospect, these pieces all share a 'conscious author' conceit. I recall struggling with each of them—and congratulating myself for diligence and, occasionally, perspicacity!

It now seems clear that they had a homelier origin, and that my prideful conscious episodes were only occasionally involved.

- Ontario Traffic Conference: "A Psychology for Traffic Enforcement", 1971.
- The Toronto Star, "Are Addicts Among Society's Sanest?", March 17, 1992.
- The Toronto Star, "Idiot factor: TV's cumulative effect", October 17, 1992.
- The Toronto Star, "Fisheries solution: negotiate", October 19, 1999.
- Municipal World, "Green Back Dollars", October, 1991.
- Kingston Whig Standard, "The Ben Johnson Story", February 8, 1990.
- The Ottawa Citizen, "Putting the jobless to work in a shadow society", November 12, 1990.
- Municipal World, "Funders Keepers—disposal of the OMERS surplus", June, 1999.
- Municipal World, "The Management vs. Union Trap", September, 1998.
- Municipal World, "Why a municipal sales tax", May, 1998.
- Municipal World, "The by-law by-law", November, 1995.

Other Projects

- *Diaspora or Oblivion: The Backlander Project* should be finished in 2017. Arguments for economic decentralization, local economies, expanding unionism to include consumers ...

- *The Colour of Angels* challenges belief systems by asking whether they are internally coherent. Even when Divine Sources are claimed, doctrinaire lives require internally-coherent axioms and principles, if only to be communicable.

- *Calculus and Evolution:* evolution demonstrates and manifests the fundamental theorem of calculus. Individuals can be understood as calculus machines integrating derivatives using genotypes and phenotypes based upon historical integrations.

The consciousness human beings are capable of creates the possibility of second, third ... order derivatives depending upon the 'cognitive capaciousness' of individuals.

http://www.backlander.ca contains material and arguments relevant to these projects. I include databases facilitating subsistence activities, local economies and group shopping.

ivanhoe@sympatico.ca

Vernon Molloy
1579 Hollowview Road,
R. R. # 1, Stirling, Ontario K0K 3E0

Index

SAVE THE WORLD

www.ingramcontent.com/pod-product-compliance
Lightning Source LLC
Chambersburg PA
CBHW061748020426
42331CB00006B/1399